# Study Guide

# CONTEMPORARY LINGUISTICS

## AN INTRODUCTION

# Study Guide

# CONTEMPORARY LINGUISTICS

## AN INTRODUCTION

### Fourth Edition

*Teresa Vanderweide*
Mount Royal College

U.S. edition prepared by

*Janie Rees-Miller*
Marietta College

*Mark Aronoff*
State University of New York at Stony Brook

Bedford/St. Martin's
Boston ♦ New York

**For Bedford/St. Martin's**

*Senior Editor:* Talvi Laev
*Senior Production Editor:* Harold Chester
*Production Supervisor:* Christie Gross
*Marketing Manager:* Richard Cadman
*Art Director:* Lucy Krikorian
*Composition:* Jan Ewing, Ewing Systems
*Printing and Binding:* Victor Graphics, Inc.

*President:* Charles H. Christensen
*Editorial Director:* Joan E. Feinberg
*Editor in Chief:* Nancy Perry
*Director of Marketing:* Karen R. Melton
*Director of Editing, Design, and Production:* Marcia Cohen
*Managing Editor:* Erica T. Appel

Library of Congress Control Number: 2001095144

Copyright © 2002 by Bedford/St. Martin's

Manufactured in the United States of America.

5  4  3  2  1
f  e  d  c  b  a

Original edition published by Pearson Education Canada Inc.,
A Pearson Education Inc. Company
Toronto, ON, Canada
Copyright © 2001 by Pearson Education Canada, Inc.

*For information, write:* Bedford/St. Martin's, 75 Arlington Street, Boston, MA 02116
(617-399-4000)

ISBN: 0-312-39710-0

# PREFACE FOR INSTRUCTORS

For some time, those of us involved in editing *Contemporary Linguistics* on the southern side of the Canadian-U.S. border have discussed the possibility of creating a workbook to accompany the text. We were, therefore, delighted when our Canadian counterparts brought out a study guide, which we have adapted here for U.S. students. More comprehensive than a simple workbook, the study guide includes not only supplementary exercises but also student-friendly summaries and reviews of important concepts found in Chapters 1–7 of *Contemporary Linguistics*. By reinforcing concepts and skills needed to understand the key areas of phonetics, phonology, morphology, syntax, semantics, and historical linguistics, the study guide helps students consolidate the foundation needed for success in the introductory linguistics course.

This study guide should prove particularly valuable for undergraduate and graduate students with no prior background in linguistics. The following features make the guide ideal for in-class use as well as independent study and review:

- Straightforward *practices,* covering the major topics in each chapter, illustrate basic linguistic processes and provide an intermediate step between learning about linguistic concepts and applying them to more challenging problems.

- Helpful *charts* guide students through the processes of setting up and solving problems.

- *Reminder boxes* provide hints where they are most needed.

- *Review exercises* for each chapter give students the opportunity to check their understanding of the chapter's concepts.

- *Recap boxes* concluding each chapter help students ensure that they have mastered important concepts and processes.

- Each chapter ends with space for students to jot down *questions* or *problems* they are encountering, or to use as scratch paper for solving practices.

- An *answer key* enables students using the guide for independent study to check their own work.

The U.S. edition of the study guide follows the organization and layout of the Canadian edition. Each chapter begins with an overview of material in the chapter; includes brief explanations, extensive exercises, and helpful reminders; and ends with a review checklist and space for noting questions or problems. For easy reference, each section in this edition is keyed to the relevant sections and pages of the fourth U.S. edition of *Contemporary Linguistics*. As in the Canadian edition, the sections labeled "advanced" in the main text are not addressed. We have Americanized spelling and language while retaining Canadian examples where they serve as well as U.S. examples. Some problems have been modified or adapted for the U.S. edition, and some are new.

This study guide has benefited from the contributions of a number of colleagues. We would like to thank Jamie Kendrioski at Marietta College for greatly improving the usability of the drawings in Chapter 2. Richard Danford and Naoko Takahashi graciously provided language data at a moment's notice. Answers supplied by Jennifer Abel, Ilana Meshewitch, and Cory Sheedy for a pilot version of the Canadian edition made our work in compiling the answer key much easier. We are grateful to Meghan Sumner at Stony Brook for her assistance in careful proofreading of the answer key. Betty Jo Chapman generously assisted in proofreading the page proofs while on vacation in Marietta. Thanks are also due to staff members of Bedford/ St. Martin's for their unfailing editorial support, particularly senior editor Talvi Laev, whose expertise and understanding have made work on the study guide a pleasure; editorial assistant Sara Billard for helping to streamline the organization of the manuscript; senior project editor Harold Chester for checking data with an eagle eye and assuring accuracy in the final stages; and production associate Christie Gross for overseeing the manuscript-to-bound-book process. The Bedford/St. Martin's staff completed the final stages of work on this study guide in the aftermath of the attack on the World Trade Center. We salute their courage and professionalism in a very difficult time.

Janie Rees-Miller
Mark Aronoff

# PREFACE TO THE CANADIAN EDITION

This workbook is intended to accompany the fourth edition of *Contemporary Linguistic Analysis*. It originally began as a series of worksheets distributed to students in class and gradually expanded to include brief explanations of text material and practice exercises, as well as review sheets. All of the material that came to be included in the workbook was either modified or designed to supplement the content found in *Contemporary Linguistic Analysis*, the text being used for introductory linguistics. As the workbook evolved, it became more generic and, as a result, potentially of use to virtually any instructor of introductory linguistics using *Contemporary Linguistic Analysis*.

The workbook contains seven chapters that correspond to the core components of linguistics: phonetics, phonology, morphology, syntax, and semantics, as well as historical linguistics. These are the main areas in which students typically require a great deal of exposure to and practice with the methods of analysis used in that particular branch of linguistics. It is hoped that this workbook will help fulfill this need. Each chapter in the workbook begins with a list of the main topics and/or concepts found within. It then contains explanations of these important concepts followed by practice exercises. All chapters include reminders of important concepts that students need to be familiar with, and conclude with a review list intended as a study guide for students. Throughout the workbook, the focus is always on the main content of the corresponding *Contemporary Linguistic Analysis* chapter: no explanations or exercises are provided for those areas of the text marked "Advanced." Finally, while every attempt was made to include as much language data as possible, the workbook does tend to emphasise Canadian English, the starting point for most students as they learn and become familiar with the methodology used in linguistic analysis.

I gratefully acknowledge contributions made by Carrie Dyck, Elaine Sorenson, Leone Sveinson, Joyce Hildebrand, and Lorna Rowsell, without whom this workbook would not have been possible. I would like to thank all the reviewers for their comments, expecially Carrie Dyck and William O'Grady for their invaluable suggestions and advice, which have improved the overall quality of the workbook. Thanks also go to Elizabeth Ritter for using a version of the workbook with her students and providing valuable feedback. Finally, I extend my sincere thanks and gratitude to Michael Dobrovolsky for his continued inspiration, support, and encouragement.

Teresa Vanderweide

# CONTENTS

Preface for Instructors     v

Preface to the Canadian Edition     vii

Contents     ix

Note to Students: How to Use This Study Guide     xi

1.  Language: A Preview     1

2.  Phonetics: The Sounds of Language     10

3.  Phonology: The Function and Patterning of Sounds     34

4.  Morphology: The Analysis of Word Structure     60

5.  Syntax: The Analysis of Sentence Structure     89

6.  Semantics: The Analysis of Meaning     113

7.  Historical Linguistics: The Study of Language Change     128

Sources     161

Answer Key     165

# NOTE TO STUDENTS:
# HOW TO USE THIS STUDY GUIDE

Welcome to the study of linguistics! For many of you using *Contemporary Linguistics* this is your first experience with the field of linguistics. Everyone speaks a language and has ideas about language, but using the analytical tools for the scientific study of language can at first seem daunting. However, with study and practice, you can discover beauty in the systematic ways in which human language behaves and be fascinated by the ways in which languages differ.

This *Study Guide* is designed to help you accomplish that goal. Since each section of the *Study Guide* is keyed to pages and sections of *Contemporary Linguistics*, you can use the relevant sections of the guide to review some of the important concepts and practice skills that you have read about in the text. For greatest benefit, we suggest the following procedure:

1. Read the appropriate section in *Contemporary Linguistics*.

2. Recall important concepts and terms, and try to explain them in your own words.

3. Read the review explanations in the *Study Guide*.

4. Work the practice problems.

5. Check your answers using the answer key in the back of the *Study Guide*.

6. List questions or difficulties on the last page of the chapter in the *Study Guide*.

7. Ask your instructor or teaching assistant for help with any difficulties and for explanations of concepts that are not clear.

This may seem like a lot of work, and it may indeed be time-consuming. However, learning the concepts and skills of a new discipline is a step-by-step process, and each step builds on the preceding one. We are confident that *Contemporary Linguistics*, complemented by this *Study Guide*, will give you the necessary foundation for understanding the principles and methods of linguistics.

# one

# LANGUAGE: A PREVIEW

The following are some of the important concepts found in this chapter. Make sure you are familiar with them.

> Specialization
> Linguistic competence
> Grammar
> Grammar generalities

## SPECIALIZATION (Section 1, pp. 1–2)

Humans are specialized for language. The characteristics below illustrate some of the aspects of our special capacity for language.

- *Speech Organs*

    Our lungs, larynx, tongue, teeth, lips, soft palate, and nasal passages are used both for survival (i.e., breathing, eating, etc.) and for producing the sounds of our language.

- *Speech Breathing*

    We have the ability to breathe not only for survival but also for speech. Speech breathing uses a different set of muscles and different lung pressure and exhalation time than our normal breathing.

- *Specialized Brain Areas*

    The human brain is structured for language. Our brains appear to have specialized areas dedicated to language production and comprehension—areas that are not found in other species.

This specialization for language sets us apart from all other creatures.

## LINGUISTIC COMPETENCE (Section 3, pp. 5–6)

Linguistic competence can be defined as a subconscious set of rules, units, and mental constructs that enables the native speakers of a language to produce and understand an unlimited number of both familiar and novel utterances.

Linguists divide the subconscious knowledge that the native speakers of a language share into the following fields of study:

1. Phonetics:      the study of the sounds found in language

2. Phonology:      the study of how sounds behave in language

3. Morphology:     the study of word structure and word formation

4. Syntax:         the study of sentence structure

5. Semantics:      the study of the meaning of words and sentences

This subconscious knowledge allows the speakers of a language to produce an infinite number of sentences, many of which we have never uttered or heard before. This is often referred to as language creativity. We don't memorize language; we create it.

While we all have this unconscious knowledge of our native language, we often make mistakes when we talk. That is, our actual use of language does not always reflect our linguistic competence.

## PRACTICE 1.1: Linguistic competence

Your linguistic competence allows you to decide whether new words and novel sentences are acceptable or not. Test your linguistic competence by answering the following questions.

1. Put a check mark beside those words that are possible English words.

   a. tlim _____        e. plog _____

   b. stuken _____      f. skpit _____

   c. tseg _____        g. ngan _____

   d. fomp_____         h. breb _____

2. Put a check mark beside those words that are possible English words.

   a. speakless _____   d. reglorify_____

   b. beautifulness _____   e. horseable _____

   c. unrug _____        f. weedic _____

   Why are some of the above not possible English words?

3.  Put a check mark beside those sentences that are possible English sentences.

    a.  The building is swept yesterday evening.     _____

    b.  The building is swept every morning.     _____

    c.  Every child should obey his parents.     _____

    d.  Somebody left their gloves in the theater.     _____

    e.  George surprised Mary with a party.     _____

    f.  Joe surprised the stone.     _____

Why are some of the above not possible English sentences?

Change this simple, and certainly not novel, sentence into a sentence that has never been spoken or written before: *The dog chased the cat.*

What did you do to create this novel sentence?

# GRAMMAR (Section 3, pp. 5–8)

Grammar, to a linguist, refers to all the elements of our linguistic competence: phonetics, phonology, morphology, syntax, and semantics. In very general terms, grammar can be defined as the system of rules and elements needed to form and interpret the sentences of a language. There are two different perspectives on grammar: prescriptive and descriptive. A prescriptive grammar gives the socially accepted rules within a language, while a descriptive grammar is an objective description of the knowledge that the native speakers of a language share.

## PRACTICE 1.2: Distinguishing prescriptive and descriptive grammar

1. Examine the boxes below (adapted from "The Verbal Edge," *Readers Digest,* August 1994), and see if you can tell which type of grammar is being exemplified.

---

WRONG:        Between you and I . . .
RIGHT:        Between you and me . . .

On an episode of the TV sitcom *Home Improvement,* handyman Tim Taylor said of competitor Bob Vila, "A lot of people think there's a big rivalry between Bob and I."

That may sound correct, but the pronoun *I* is wrong here. *Between* is a preposition, and prepositions are always followed by objects. *I* is a subject or nominative pronoun. So are *he, she, we,* and *they.* Objective pronouns that follow a preposition are *me, you, him, her, us,* and *them.*

Use the rhyme "Between thee and me" as a reminder.

WRONG:        She is older than me.
RIGHT:        She is older than I.

Unlike *between,* the word *than* is not a preposition; it's a conjunction—a word that joins two sentence, words, or phrases. In this case there are two sentences: (1) *She is older* and (2) *I am*—but the *am* has been dropped, and that throws people off.

In a comparison joined by *than* or *as,* just complete the sentence, and the correct word will be obvious. You wouldn't say "He is smarter than me am," so it must be *He is smarter than I.*

---

WRONG:        Who do I ask?
RIGHT:        Whom do I ask?

*Who* and *whom* will never stump you if you remember: *Who* is generally appropriate whenever you use *he, she,* or *they; whom* acts as a substitute for *him, her,* or *them.* Sometimes it helps to recast a question into a statement. In this example, you'd never say "I ask he," so the correct wording is *Whom do I ask?* ("But that sounds stuffy," you say. Yes—which is why the incorrect *Who do I ask?* is sometimes used in informal situations.)

WRONG:        The demand for durable goods such as cars and home appliances were unchanged last month.
RIGHT:        The demand for durable goods such as cars and home appliances was unchanged last month.

A CNN news anchor delivered this blooper, which goes to show that even professionals err. The mistake was mating a plural verb with a singular subject. And it often happens as it did here: the subject of the sentence, *demand,* was singular, but it got separated from the verb by the plural phrase *such as cars and home appliances.* Distracted by these particulars, the anchor forgot that she was speaking in the singular and used a plural verb. Keep your mind on the subject—what it is you're talking about.

---

The above are all examples of a prescriptivist view on language. While a prescriptivist grammar is useful in helping people learn a foreign language in that it contains the socially accepted rules for language use, linguists are more interested in descriptive grammar.

2. Each of the following aspects of linguistic competence contains two statements. See if you can identify which statement is prescriptivist and which is descriptivist. Do this by writing either P.G. (prescriptive grammar) or D.G. (descriptive grammar) beside each statement.

a.  Sounds

_____  The English words *Mary, merry,* and *marry* should be pronounced differently because they are spelled differently.

_____  English contains over twenty different consonant sounds.

How many different vowel sounds are found in English?

Do all languages have the same consonant and/or vowel sounds? Think of a language that has different consonant or vowel sounds.

b.  Words

_____  The use of *has went* instead of *has gone* is an example of how change is causing the English language to deteriorate.

_____  Many nouns in English are formed by adding the suffix *-ment* to words (e.g., *achievement, government, judgment*).

Why would no English speaker construct the word *chairment*?

c.  Sentences

_____  There are at least two ways in English to make a sentence refer to the future.

_____  The auxiliary *shall* should be used with first person (i.e., *I, we*), whereas *will* should be used for second and third persons (e.g., *He will go, but we shall stay*).

Revise the following sentence in two different ways to make it refer to the future: *The horses eat hay.*

How do other languages make statements refer to future time?

d. Meaning

_____ The word *cool* should only be used to refer to temperature.

_____ Words often come in pairs of opposites (e.g., *hot/cold, light/dark*).

How is the meaning of a sentence different from the meaning of the words that compose it?

---

**REMINDER**

Linguistics is the study of the structure of human language, and linguists attempt to describe in an objective and nonjudgmental fashion the internalized and unconscious knowledge that the native speakers of a language share, and that allows them to both speak and understand their language. While the primary focus of this guide is on English, many of the principles and theories discussed apply to all other languages as well.

# GRAMMAR GENERALITIES (Sections 3.1–3.5, pp. 6–11)

While at first glance, languages appear to be very different from one another, there are actually many similarities across languages. Some known facts about language include the following:

- *Generality: All languages have a grammar*

  All languages have sounds, words, sentences, and meaning. Therefore, all languages have a grammar. Different languages and different varieties of the same language simply have different grammars.

- *Parity: All grammars are equal*

  All languages and varieties of language allow for the expression of any thought. Therefore, one grammar is no better or worse than any other grammar. Similarly, there are no inferior or primitive languages. Remember, linguists attempt to describe grammars, not prescribe the "correct" way of using grammar.

- *Universality: All grammars are alike in basic ways*

  All languages share common principles and tendencies called universals. Languages, of course, do differ from one another. However, even the variation that exists between languages is limited. Linguists use parameters to describe this limited variation.

- *Mutability: All grammars change over time*

  The grammars of all languages change over time. New words are constantly being added, and over time even the word order of a language can change. However, contrary to a prescriptivist viewpoint, change does not cause a language to deteriorate.

- *Inaccessibility: Grammatical knowledge is subconscious*

  All native speakers of a language have knowledge of its grammar. And this knowledge is subconscious and was acquired as a child without formal instruction. This unconscious knowledge allows us to use language without having to think too much about how to put a sentence together.

## REVIEW EXERCISE

Each of the following statements illustrates a concept covered in Chapter 1. For each statement, determine which concept is being illustrated. Do this by writing the number of the concept beside each statement. The first one is done for you.

**Concepts:**
1. Linguistic competence
2. Prescriptive grammar
3. Descriptive grammar
4. Universality

**Statements:**

a. _____4_____ All languages have a way of making negatives.

b. _____ Speakers of American English know that one way to make questions is to move an auxiliary verb ahead of the subject noun phrase.

c. _____ Many nouns in English are formed by adding -*ness* to an adjective, for example: *sadness, silliness,* and *happiness*.

d. _____ *Brung* should never be used as the past tense of *bring*.

e. _____ Every language has a set of vowels and consonants.

f. _____ Speakers of any language are capable of producing an unlimited number of novel sentences.

g. _____ In English, there is no theoretical limit on the number of adjectives that can occur before a noun.

h. _____ In the sentence *My friend is smarter than me, me* is incorrect because it is an object pronoun and this comparative construction requires the subject pronoun *I*.

i. _____ In English, the plural is formed by adding [-s], [-z], or [-əz] to the end of nouns.

j. _____ Every language has a way of forming questions.

k. _____ Speakers of American English know that the different vowel sounds in the words *bat, bet, but,* and *bit* are crucial to their meanings.

☑ **RECAP**

Make sure you understand these terms. (See also the Key Terms on p. 11 of the main text.)

- creativity
- descriptive grammar
- generality
- grammar
- inaccessibility
- linguistic competence
- mutability
- native speaker
- parity
- prescriptive grammar

- specialized brain areas
- speech breathing
- speech organs
- universality

## QUESTIONS? PROBLEMS?

# two

# PHONETICS: THE SOUNDS OF LANGUAGE

Phonetics is the study of the articulation and perception of speech sounds. Following are some of the important topics and concepts covered in this chapter. Make sure you are familiar with them.

[vowkəl trækt]
[sawnd klæsəz]
[artʰɪkjulətɔri dɪskrɪpʃənz]
[plejsez əv artʰɪkjulejʃən]
[əmɛrəkən kʰansənənts]
[æspərejʃən]
[fejʃəl dajəgræmz]
[əmɛrəkən vawəlz]
[sɛgmənts]
[trænskrɪpʃən]
[ʃɛrd fənɛtɪk prapərtiz]
[suprəsɛgmɛntəlz]
[prasɛsəz]

Don't worry. By the end of this section, you'll be able to translate the above phonetic transcription into standard English with ease.

In "plain" English, some of the topics we will be discussing in phonetics are:

Vocal tract
Sound classes
Articulatory descriptions
Places of articulation
American English consonants
Aspiration
Facial diagrams
American English vowels
Segments
Transcription
Shared phonetic properties
Suprasegmentals
Processes

## THE VOCAL TRACT (Section 2, pp. 18–21)

The vocal tract is the sound-producing system. It includes the lungs, trachea, larynx, pharynx, velum, oral cavity, and nasal cavity. Speech sounds are made as air passes through the vocal tract.

### PRACTICE 2.1: Parts of the vocal tract

On the following diagram, label the lungs, trachea, esophagus, larynx, pharynx, oral cavity, nasal cavity, and velum.

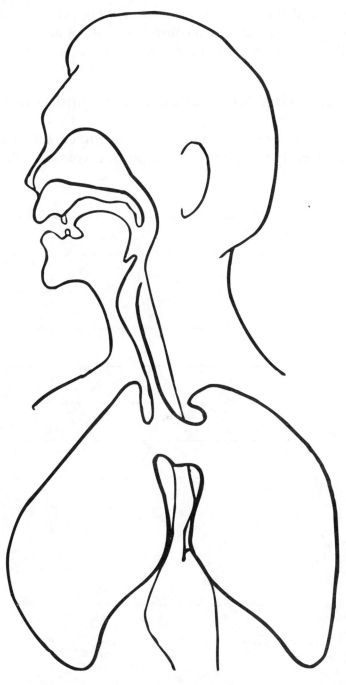

## SOUND CLASSES (Section 3, pp. 21–22)

Sounds produced with the vocal tract can be divided into three major classes: consonants, vowels, and glides. The defining characteristics of each class are given below.

- **Consonants.** Consonantal sounds are made with a narrow or complete obstruction in the vocal tract. Some of them come in voiced/voiceless pairs.

- **Vowels.** Vowel sounds are made with little obstruction in the vocal tract, and are typically voiced. Vowels tend to be more sonorous than consonants. Vowels are also classified as syllabic sounds, meaning that they can function as the nucleus of a syllable.

- **Glides.** Glides are sounds that have characteristics of both consonants and vowels. They are sometimes called semivowels or semiconsonants. Glides are like vowels in their articulation, but are like consonants in that they do not function as the nucleus of a syllable.

### PRACTICE 2.2: Identifying consonants, vowels, and glides

Each of the following words has one or more letters underlined. The underlined letters correspond to one sound. Identify this sound as a consonant, vowel, or glide. The first is done for you.

1. rott<u>w</u>eiler     _consonant_

2. thr<u>ough</u>

3. <u>l</u>ovely

4. <u>y</u>ear

5. my<u>th</u>

6. <u>wh</u>istle

7. su<u>ff</u>er

8. ju<u>dge</u>

# ARTICULATORY DESCRIPTIONS

All sounds, regardless of whether they are consonants, vowels, or glides, are described in terms of how they are articulated. This information is contained in the sound's articulatory description. Every sound has one and only one articulatory description. Every articulatory description corresponds to one symbol in the International Phonetic Alphabet (IPA). Consonants and glides are described differently than vowels.

## Consonant Articulation (Sections 2.3, 4, 5)

There are three parameters necessary to describe consonant (and glide) articulation:

- Glottal state (Section 2.3, pp. 19–21)
- Place of articulation (Section 4.2, pp. 23–24)
- Manner of articulation (Section 5, pp. 25–32)

Glottal state refers to whether a sound is voiced or voiceless. Place of articulation refers to where in the vocal tract an obstruction occurs. Manner of articulation refers to how the airflow is modified at the place of articulation.

## Vowel Articulation (Section 6)

Four parameters are necessary to describe vowels: (Sections 6.2–6.3, pp. 33–36)

- Tongue height
- Tongue position
- Tenseness
- Lip position

Tongue height and tongue position are used to describe tongue placement. Tenseness refers to the amount of constriction in the vocal tract muscles when the sound is articulated. Lip position refers to whether the lips are rounded.

---

## REMINDER

For every articulatory description, you need to be able to provide the corresponding phonetic symbol, for example:

voiceless bilabial stop     →     [p]

For every phonetic symbol, you need to be able to provide the corresponding articulatory description, for example:

[ej]     →     mid front tense unrounded vowel

---

## PLACES OF ARTICULATION (Section 4.2, pp. 23–24)

Different places in the vocal tract can be modified to produce different sounds. Most of these places are found within the oral cavity, but there are two places of articulation outside the oral cavity.

### PRACTICE 2.3: Locating places of articulation

On the following diagram, identify all the places of articulation within the oral cavity as well as the two places of articulation outside the oral cavity.

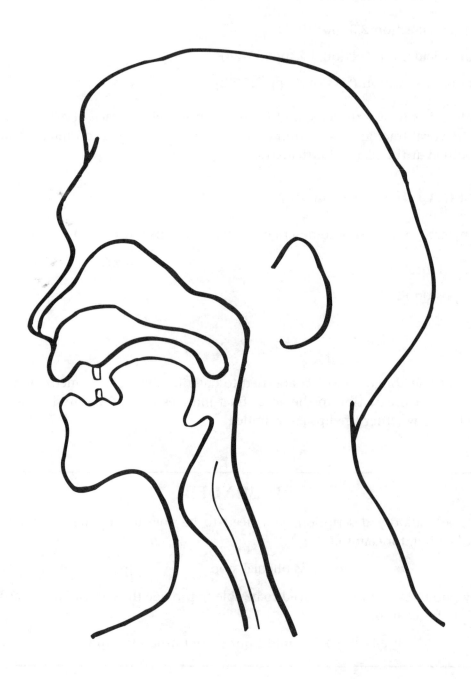

# AMERICAN ENGLISH CONSONANT CHART

Consonant sounds are classified according to:

- where they are articulated (place of articulation)
- how they are articulated (manner of articulation)
- whether they are voiced or voiceless (glottal state)

Although the consonant chart looks daunting, you will find that completing it will help you remember each phonetic symbol.

## PRACTICE 2.4: Consonants

Fill in the chart with the symbols corresponding to the consonant and glide sounds of American English.

| | | GLOTTAL STATE | PLACE OF ARTICULATION | | | | | | | |
|---|---|---|---|---|---|---|---|---|---|---|
| | | | Bilabial | Labiodental | Interdental | Alveolar | Alveopalatal | Palatal | Velar | Glottal |
| M A N N E R  O F  A R T I C U L A T I O N | Stop | voiceless | | | | | | | | |
| | | voiced | | | | | | | | |
| | Fricative | voiceless | | | | | | | | |
| | | voiced | | | | | | | | |
| | Affricate | voiceless | | | | | | | | |
| | | voiced | | | | | | | | |
| | Nasal | voiced | | | | | | | | |
| | Liquid a. lateral | voiced | | | | | | | | |
| | b. retroflex | voiced | | | | | | | | |
| | Glide | voiced | | | | | | | | |

## ASPIRATION (Section 5.5, pp. 28–30)

Sometimes when voiceless stops are pronounced, they are produced with a small puff of air. This puff of air is called aspiration and is represented as [ ʰ ]. Pronounce the words in the boxes below, paying close attention to the first sound, and see if you can tell when aspiration does and does not occur. You can feel this extra release of air by putting your hand close to your mouth as you produce the words. (It is easier to feel the puff of air with bilabial and alveolar stops than with the velar stop.)

| ASPIRATED VOICELESS STOPS | |
|---|---|
| [pʰ] | pit<br>punk |
| [tʰ] | take<br>tab |
| [kʰ] | kill<br>car |

| UNASPIRATED VOICELESS STOPS | |
|---|---|
| [p] | spit<br>spunk |
| [t] | stake<br>stab |
| [k] | skill<br>scar |

Voiceless stops in English can be both aspirated and unaspirated. Aspiration occurs only when there is a delay in the voicing of the vowel after the voiceless stop. This delay occurs in words such as *pit, take,* and *kill* because there is not enough time after the release of the voiceless stop to vibrate the vocal folds for the vowel articulation. The vowel therefore is not immediately voiced, and it is this initial voicelessness that is perceived as a puff of air. In words such as *spit, stake,* and *skill,* there is no delay in voicing, and therefore no aspiration. The delay does not occur because the presence of an extra sound provides the time necessary to get the vocal folds into position to immediately start voicing the vowel when the stop is released.

### PRACTICE 2.5: Aspiration

Pronounce the following words, and put a check mark beside those words containing aspirated voiceless stops.

1. scratch _____

2. talk _____

3. segments _____

4. pending _____

5. stripe _____

6. careful _____

# FACIAL DIAGRAMS

There are four important parts to completing or deciphering facial diagrams.

**Voicing/Voicelessness.** Voiceless sounds are represented by two lines shaped like an ellipse. Voiced sounds are shown by two wavy lines where the larynx would be.

**Nasal Passage.** For oral sounds, the nasal passage is closed; for nasal sounds, the nasal passage is open.

VOICELESS, ORAL

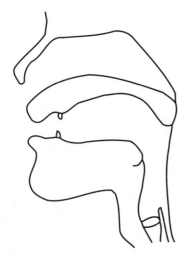

VOICED, NASAL

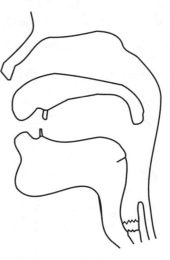

**Place of Articulation.** The narrowest point in the airstream passage is the place of articulation.

**Manner of Articulation.** If no air escapes past a given articulator (i.e., a stop), then the articulator must touch the place of articulation. If the air does escape (i.e., a fricative), then there is a space between the articulator and the place of articulation. If the sound is an affricate, then the diagram is shown with the articulator touching the place of articulation and an arrow indicating the direction in which the articulator moves.

STOP

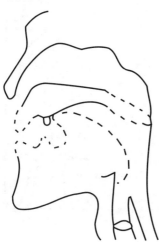

FRICATIVE

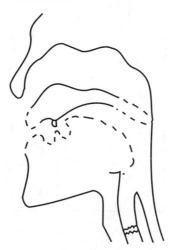

AFFRICATE

## PRACTICE 2.6: Drawing facial diagrams

Complete the following diagrams so that each of the sounds listed below is depicted.

1.   [ s ]           3.   [ dʒ ]           5.   [ g ]
2.   [ b ]           4.   [ n ]            6.   [ ð ]

To complete the diagrams, you must:

- Draw in the lips: either closed or open.
- Draw the tongue to the place of articulation and to the manner of articulation.
- Draw in the velum: either closed or open.
- Draw in the glottis: either open or vibrating.

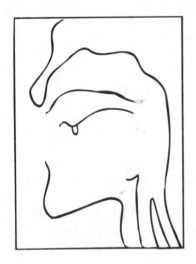
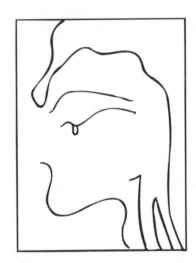
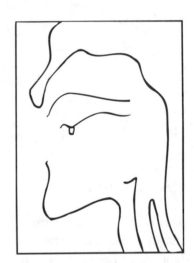

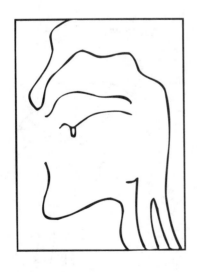
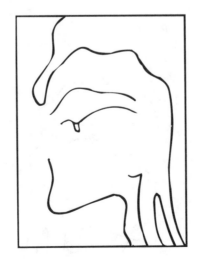
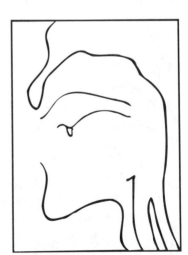

## PRACTICE 2.7: Reading facial diagrams

For each of the following drawings, there is only one sound that could be produced by the vocal tract position. Figure out which consonant sound is represented, and write the phonetic symbol for that sound between the brackets below the drawing.

Make sure that you pay attention to voicing, to place and manner of articulation, and to the position of the velum.

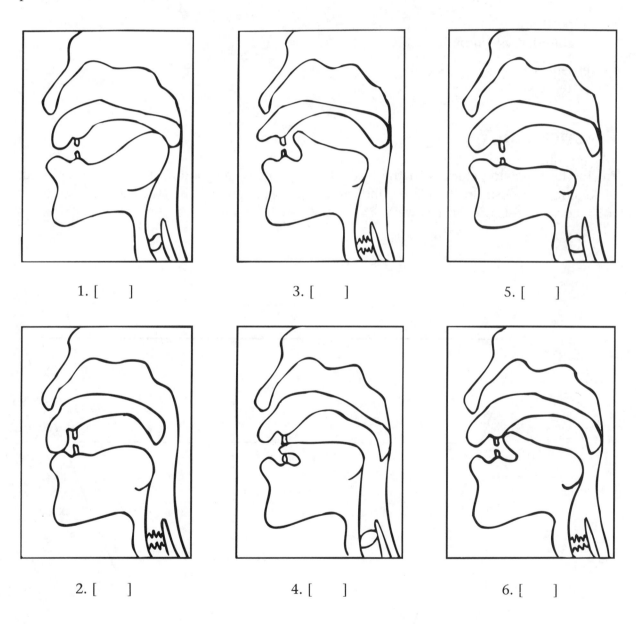

1. [     ]        3. [     ]        5. [     ]

2. [     ]        4. [     ]        6. [     ]

# AMERICAN ENGLISH VOWEL CHART

Vowels are classified according to:

- tongue height:
    high vs. mid vs. low

- tongue position:
    front vs. (central vs.) back

- lip position:
    rounded vs. unrounded

- tenseness:
    tense vs. lax

## PRACTICE 2.8: Vowels

Fill in the following chart with the phonetic symbols corresponding to the vowel sounds of American English. In the blanks, indicate tongue position and height. Label the group of rounded vowels. Circle tense vowels.

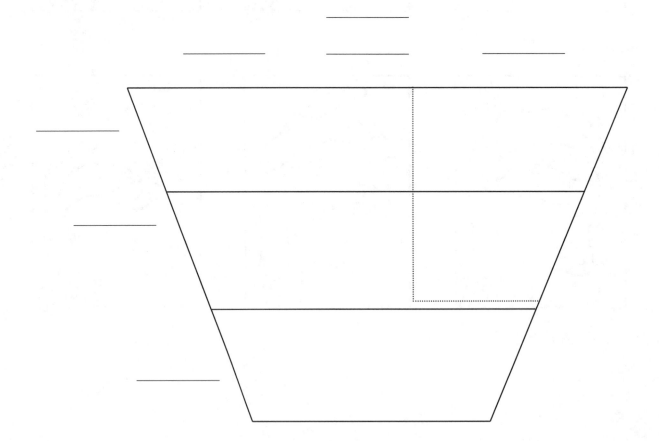

## SEGMENTS (Section 1, pp. 16–17)

To transcribe words successfully, you need to be able to identify individual sounds. An individual speech sound (or phone) is called a segment, and each segment is represented by a symbol in the phonetic alphabet. Words typically consist of a number of different speech sounds. To transcribe, you need to determine not only the number of speech sounds in a word but also what those speech sounds are. But don't be fooled by spelling. Each of the following boxes illustrates a reason why we can't rely on spelling to determine the number of speech sounds in an English word.

---

Some letters or combinations of letters have more than one speech sound associated with them. In each of the following example sets, determine if the underlined letter(s) are pronounced the same way for all the words presented.

1. 'o' as in h<u>o</u>t ech<u>o</u> w<u>o</u>man

2. 'c' as in <u>c</u>areful <u>c</u>entury <u>c</u>ello

3. 'ou' as in sh<u>ou</u>ld t<u>ou</u>gh s<u>ou</u>nd

---

Sometimes one speech sound can be represented using different letters or combinations of letters. In each of the following example sets, determine if the underlined letter(s) have the same or different speech sounds.

1. thr<u>ough</u> cl<u>ue</u> sh<u>oe</u> t<u>oo</u>

2. r<u>ea</u>l s<u>ee</u> sorr<u>y</u> Sh<u>ei</u>la

3. str<u>aw</u> t<u>a</u>lk f<u>ou</u>ght l<u>o</u>st

---

Many words in English contain double letters. Double letters do not necessarily mean that there are two speech sounds. Say each of the following words and determine if the doubled letter is pronounced twice.

str<u>ee</u>t b<u>oo</u>k mi<u>tt</u>en ki<u>ll</u>er

---

Finally, many words in English contain silent letters. These are letters that are not pronounced and that therefore do not correspond to a speech sound. Say each of the following words, and determine if all of the letters are pronounced.

knife leave pneumonia catch

---

The lesson is: When you are transcribing words, you need to forget about spelling.

## PRACTICE 2.9: Segments and phonetic symbols

To get ready for transcription, try the following exercises.

1.  Determine the number of speech sounds in each of the following words. Count dipthongs as single sounds.

    a.  thing _____

    b.  comb _____

    c.  psychic _____

    d.  phosphate _____

    e.  scene _____

    f.  fright _____

2.  Give the phonetic symbol for the first sound in each of the following words.

    a.  Thomas _____

    b.  unemployed _____

    c.  committee _____

    d.  knee _____

    e.  choice _____

    f.  ease _____

3.  Give the phonetic symbol for the last sound in each of the following words.

    a.  laugh _____

    b.  sang _____

    c.  bow _____

    d.  lamb _____

    e.  use _____

    f.  choice _____

## [trænskrɪpʃən tajm]    (Section 1, pp. 16–17; Section 7, pp. 36–38)

## Syllabic Consonants

| r | [r] for the 'r' sound in *real, right,* etc.<br>[ər], [r̩], or [ɚ] for the syllabic 'r' sound in *butter, bird, purr,* etc.<br>[ɾ] for the 't' sound in *butter, writer, putter, potter,* etc. |
|---|---|
| l | [l] for the 'l' sound in *light, pill, please,* etc.<br>[əl] or [l̩] for the syllabic 'l' in *bottle, puddle, poodle,* etc. |
| m | [m̩] for the syllabic 'm' in *bottom, winsome,* etc.<br>[m] for any other 'm' sound |
| n | [n̩] for the syllabic 'n' in *button, hidden,* etc.<br>[n] for any other 'n' sound |

## Vowels

The mid tense vowels have an off-glide in phonetic transcription only:

| phonetic transcription: | [ej], [ow] |
|---|---|
| phonemic transcription: | /e/, /o/ |

Vowels before [r]:

| [bir] | beer | [bɔr] | boar | [bejr] | bear | | |
|---|---|---|---|---|---|---|---|
| [bɑr] | bar | [bur] | boor | [bər], [br̩], or [bɚ] | | burr | |

## Schwa and Wedge

| Schwa [ə] | Wedge [ʌ] |
|---|---|
| • used for unstressed vowels<br>    [əbawt]  about<br>• found before [r]<br>    [bərd]  bird<br>• used for the words *the* and *a* | • used when there is some degree of<br>stress on the vowel<br>    [sʌpər]  supper<br>• is not found before [r] |

## Aspiration

| p, t, k | use [pʰ, tʰ, kʰ] for any 'p', 't', 'k' sound that occurs at the beginning of a syllable followed by a vowel that receives some degree of stress.<br>[pʰæt] pat,  [tʰɔt] taught,  [kʰejk] cake<br>[əpʰˈir] appear,  [ətʰǽk] attack |
|---|---|
| | Use [p, t, k] for any other 'p', 't', 'k' sound.<br>[splæt] splat,  [stɑp] stop,  [skejt] skate |

## Canadian Raising

Most dialects in the U.S. do not have Canadian raising, although some do.

| Phonetic Transcription:<br><br>[aj] and [aw] before voiced consonants or when not followed by any consonant<br>    [bajd], [laj] bide and lie,  [lawd], [baw] loud and bough<br>[ʌy] and [ʌw] before voiceless consonants<br>    [bʌjt] bite,  [lʌwt] lout |
|---|
| Phonemic Transcription:   /aj/ and /aw/ in all environments |

## PRACTICE 2.10: [trænskrɪpʃən ɛksɾsajzəz]

Transcribe the following words as you would say them in normal everyday speech. Remember to include brackets and remember to forget spelling. Watch out for syllabic consonants.

1. craft _____
2. sigh _____
3. health _____
4. azure _____
5. frog _____
6. paddle _____
7. angel _____

8. rich _____
9. tape _____
10. vague _____
11. rooster _____
12. instead _____
13. bottom _____
14. church _____

15. thought _____
16. had _____
17. exit _____
18. sugar _____
19. unit _____
20. question _____

## PRACTICE 2.11: Transcribing vowels

Remember that the tense mid vowels have an off-glide in phonetic transcription.

1. key _____        5. cheese _____        9. bone _____

2. due _____        6. ate _____        10. east _____

3. loaf _____        7. wheeze _____        11. baby _____

4. made _____        8. through _____        12. throw _____

## PRACTICE 2.12: Transcribing vowels before [r]

This time watch out for vowels before [r] sounds.

1. cheer _____        7. there _____        13. chair _____

2. car _____        8. star _____        14. score _____

3. sir _____        9. her _____        15. floor _____

4. oar _____        10. horse _____        16. course _____

5. heart _____        11. hard _____        17. harm _____

6. sharp _____        12. shirt _____        18. thwart _____

## PRACTICE 2.13: Diphthongs

Transcribe the following words as you would in normal everyday speech. Watch out for those diphthongs.

1. voice _____        7. trial _____        13. bicycle _____

2. hour _____        8. oily _____        14. price _____

3. eyes _____        9. prize _____        15. embroider _____

4. sight _____        10. sigh _____        16. sighed _____

5. prowl _____        11. counter _____        17. ice _____

6. knifed _____        12. down _____        18. daze _____

Remember . . . transcription takes a lot of practice.

## PRACTICE 2.14: Schwa and wedge

For this group, pay close attention to the schwa and wedge sounds. You might want to determine which vowel gets primary stress to help you out.

1. sludge _____
2. quality _____
3. luck _____
4. nation _____

5. thunder _____
6. behave _____
7. separate _____
8. announce _____

9. hung _____
10. oven _____
11. stuff _____
12. understand _____

## PRACTICE 2.15: Reading transcription

Give the correctly spelled English word for each of the following transcriptions.

1. [liʒər] _____
2. [æks] _____
3. [wərði] _____
4. [wʌns] _____
5. [ʃejd] _____

6. [ʃaj] _____
7. [swit] _____
8. [tʰub] _____
9. [ʧɔjs] _____
10. [mɛnʃən] _____

11. [pʰajp] _____
12. [sɔfənd] _____
13. [fowni] _____
14. [stæʧu] _____
15. [skwɛr] _____

# SHARED PHONETIC PROPERTIES

Sounds are distinguished by their phonetic properties, but they can also share phonetic properties. Phonetic properties include such things as voice, place of articulation, manner of articulation, tongue height, and lip position.

## PRACTICE 2.16: Shared phonetic properties

Each of the following groups of sounds contains at least one shared phonetic property. For each group of sounds, state the phonetic properties that the sounds have in common. Include as many as possible. The first is done for you.

1. [ b, d, g ]     _____voiced stops_____

2. [ v, d, m ]     _____

3. [ s, ʧ, ʒ ]     _____

4. [ j, ɾ, n ]    _____

5. [ ɑ, o, ʊ ]    _____

6. [ æ, ɪ, ɛ ]    _____

Groups of sounds that share phonetic properties are called natural classes.

# SUPRASEGMENTALS (Section 8, pp. 38–43)

Suprasegmentals refer to inherent properties that are part of all sounds regardless of their place or manner of articulation. The three main suprasegmentals are pitch, length, and stress. Pitch is further divided into tone and intonation.

- **Pitch.** Tone languages are languages in which pitch movement is used to signal differences in meaning. Mandarin Chinese is a good example. Intonation is pitch movement that is not related to differences in word meaning. For example, rising pitch is often used to signal a question.

- **Length.** Long vowels and consonants are sounds whose articulation simply takes longer relative to other vowels and consonants. Length is indicated with a [ ː ] following the segment.

- **Stress.** Stress is associated with vowels. Stressed vowels are vowels that are perceived as more prominent than other vowels. The most prominent vowel receives primary stress. Primary stress is usually indicated with a [ ´ ] placed over the vowel.

# PROCESSES (Section 9, pp. 43–50)

Processes describe articulatory adjustments that occur during speech. Processes typically function to make words easier to articulate. Processes also occur to make speech easier to perceive. The main types of processes are:

- Assimilation
- Dissimilation
- Deletion
- Epenthesis
- Metathesis
- Vowel reduction

The following boxes define and illustrate the different processes found in language.

## Assimilation

Assimilation involves sounds changing to become more like nearby sounds. While there are many different kinds of assimilation, in general, assimilation can be divided into three main types:

1. Assimilation for voice:
     A sound takes on the same voice as a nearby sound.
     Includes: voicing, devoicing.

2. Assimilation for place of articulation:
     A sound takes on the same place of articulation as a nearby sound.
     Includes: palatalization, homorganic nasal assimilation, and more.

3. Assimilation for manner of articulation:
     A sound takes on the same manner of articulation as a nearby sound.
     Includes: nasalization, flapping (tapping), and more.

*Note:* Some types of assimilation, such as nasalization, can be either regressive or progressive. In regressive assimilation, a segment takes on some characteristic of the following segment. That is, a sound is influenced by what comes after it. In progressive assimilation, a segment takes on some characteristic of the preceding segment. That is, a sound is influenced by what comes before it.

## Dissimilation

A sound changes to become less like a nearby sound so that the resulting sequence of sounds is easier to pronounce.

## Deletion

The process of deletion simply removes a sound from a phonetic context. Deletion frequently occurs in rapid speech.

## Epenthesis

The process of epenthesis adds a segment to a phonetic context. Epenthesis is common in casual speech.

## Metathesis

Metathesis is a process that changes the order of segments. Metathesis is common in the speech of young children.

## Vowel Reduction

In vowel reduction, vowels move to a more central position when they are in unstressed syllables. That is, a vowel is pronounced as a full vowel when in a stressed syllable, and as a schwa when in an unstressed syllable.

**Identifying processes:** To identify processes, you need to look for differences between the starting and the ending pronunciation.

- If a sound is missing, **deletion** has occurred.

- If a sound has been added, **epenthesis** has occurred.

- If the order of sounds has changed, **metathesis** has occurred.

- If a sound has changed, you need to determine if either **assimilation** or **dissimilation** has occurred. To do this, follow these four steps:

  1. Determine the phonetic property that has changed (voice, place of articulation, or manner of articulation).
  2. Compare this phonetic property with the phonetic properties of the nearby sounds.
  3. If the changed phonetic property matches a phonetic property of a nearby sound, then **assimilation** has occurred. The phonetic property that matches will tell you the specific type of assimilation that has occurred.
  4. If the phonetic properties do not match, then **dissimilation** has occurred.

**Remember:** For assimilation, you also need to be able to identify when processes such as nasalization or place of articulation are regressive and when they are progressive. To determine this, you need to look at whether the influencing sound comes before (progressive) or after (regressive) the sound that is undergoing the change.

Consider the following example.

$$\text{prince:} \quad [\text{prɪns}] \quad \rightarrow \quad [\text{prɪ̃nts}]$$

In the above example, [t] occurs in the final pronunciation but not the starting; therefore, epenthesis has occurred. As well, [ɪ] has changed to [ɪ̃]. Remember that [˜] indicates a nasalized sound. The vowel has therefore changed from an oral to a nasal sound, and since the following sound is a nasal, assimilation—in particular, nasalization—has occurred. The influencing sound is the following nasal, meaning that the nasalization is regressive. So, the change in the pronunciation of the word *prince* from [prɪns] to [prɪ̃nts] involves two processes: epenthesis and regressive nasalization.

### PRACTICE 2.17: Identifying processes

Identify the process(es) at work in each of the following:

1. sibilant:    [sɪbələnt]    →    [sɪləbənt]    _____

2. Peter:    [pʰitər]    →    [pʰiɾər]    _____

3. puddle:    [pʰʌdl̩]    →    [pʰʌɾl̩]    _____

4. good-bye:    [gʊdbaj]    →    [gõmbaj]    _____

5. sixths:    [sɪksθs]    →    [sɪksts]    _____

# REVIEW EXERCISES

1. For each part of the vocal tract, give its corresponding role in speech production.

    a. lungs    _____

    b. larynx    _____

    c. velum    _____

2. Give the articulatory term describing sounds made at each of the following places of articulation.

    a. lips    _____

    b. hard palate    _____

    c. uvula    _____

    d. larynx    _____

3. Give the phonetic symbol for each of the following articulatory descriptions.

    a. [   ]    voiceless glottal stop

    b. [   ]    high front unrounded tense vowel

    c. [   ]    voiced bilabial nasal

    d. [   ]    voiceless interdental fricative

4. Give the articulatory description that corresponds to each of the following phonetic symbols.

    a. [ æ ]    _____

b.  [ v ]  _____

c.  [ j ]  _____

d.  [ ʌ ]  _____

5.  Give the phonetic symbol for the vowel sound in each of the following English words.

a.  stool  _____          d.  pot  _____

b.  sight  _____          e.  sit _____

c.  meet  _____          f.  put  _____

6.  Transcribe the following words as you would say them in normal everyday speech. Mark primary stress.

a.  scorned  _____          f.  duplicate  _____

b.  discovery  _____          g.  dictate_____

c.  explosion  _____          h.  occupied_____

d.  genius  _____          i.  informative  _____

e.  macaroni  _____          j.  idolize_____

7.  Transcribe the following words as you would say them in normal everyday speech. Pay special attention to vowels. Watch out; they get harder.

| | | | | | |
|---|---|---|---|---|---|
| 1.  days | _____ | 11.  agitate | _____ | 21.  gnome | _____ |
| 2.  Xerox | _____ | 12.  roast | _____ | 22.  sixths | _____ |
| 3.  guess | _____ | 13.  thumb | _____ | 23.  masculine | _____ |
| 4.  yellow | _____ | 14.  bargain | _____ | 24.  precious | _____ |
| 5.  science | _____ | 15.  machine | _____ | 25.  formula | _____ |
| 6.  motorcycle | _____ | 16.  surrounded | _____ | 26.  comedy | _____ |
| 7.  extinguish | _____ | 17.  costume | _____ | 27.  graduate | _____ |
| 8.  implement | _____ | 18.  writer | _____ | 28.  irrigate | _____ |
| 9.  isolate | _____ | 19.  timetable | _____ | 29.  unforgivable | _____ |
| 10.  frighten | _____ | 20.  lemonade | _____ | 30.  called | _____ |

8.  For each of the following groups of sounds, circle the sound that does not belong and state a phonetic property that the remaining sounds share. There may be more than one possible answer.

    a.  [ f ð v m ]  _____

    b.  [ d t n g ]  _____

    c.  [ ɑ o ɪ u ]  _____

9.  Identify all the processes at work in each of the following:

    a.  wash:      [wɔʃ]  →  [wɔrʃ]      _____

    b.  winter:    [wɪntər]  →  [wĩnər]      _____

    c.  clear:     [kl̥ir]  →  [kəlir]      _____

    d.  sandwich:  [sændwɪtʃ]  →  [sæ̃mwɪtʃ]      _____

    e.  animal:    [ænɪməl]  →  [æmɪnəl]      _____

**RECAP**

Make sure you know the following material. (See also the Key Terms on pp. 54–56 of the main text.)

- the different parts of the vocal tract
- the difference between voiced and voiceless sounds
- the difference between nasal and oral sounds
- the characteristics of consonants, glides, and vowels
- the places and manners of articulation for consonant sounds
- the different tongue placements required to describe vowels
- the difference between tense and lax, and rounded and unrounded vowels
- the symbols and articulatory descriptions for English consonants
- the strident fricatives and affricates
- the symbols and articulatory descriptions for English vowels
- when and why aspiration occurs
- how to complete and decipher facial diagrams
- how to identify natural classes
- how to identify processes
- the suprasegmentals of tone, intonation, length, and stress
- transcription

## QUESTIONS? PROBLEMS?

*three*

# PHONOLOGY: THE FUNCTION AND PATTERNING OF SOUNDS

Phonology is the study of how sounds vary and pattern in language. Following are some of the improtant topics and concepts covered in this chapter. Make sure you are familiar with them.

| | |
|---|---|
| Phonemes and allophones | Phonetic and phonemic transcription |
| Minimal pairs | Syllables |
| Complementary distribution | Features |
| Phonology problems | Rules and statements |
| Near-minimal pairs and free variation | Derivations and rule-ordering |

Since we will be dealing with many languages besides English, you will come across some phonetic symbols that have not yet been discussed. Articulatory descriptions will be provided for these unfamiliar sounds.

## PHONEMES AND ALLOPHONES (Section 2.2, pp. 69–71)

Phonemes and allophones are two units of representation used in phonology. These are used to capture native-speaker knowledge about how sounds behave in that language.

Phoneme refers to:

- the way in which the sounds are stored in the mind
- all "members" of the language's sound system
- underlying representation

Allophone refers to:

- the way in which the sounds are pronounced
- the individual members of the language's sound system
- surface representation

---

### REMINDER

Don't forget that phonemes are indicated with slashes / / and allophones with brackets [ ].

---

## MINIMAL PAIRS (Sections 1.1–1.2, pp. 65–68)

Minimal pairs are defined as two phonetic forms that differ by one segment that is in the same position in both forms, and which causes the forms to have different meanings. Minimal pairs tell us that sounds contrast.

### PRACTICE 3.1: Recognizing minimal pairs

For each of the following, answer Yes if the paired words constitute a minimal pair and No if they do not. Make sure you pay attention to the meanings given in single quotation marks.

1.  [bækt]  'towel'  and  [pækd]  'cloth'  _____

2.  [ʧogʊr]  'necklace'  and  [ʧogʊl]  'bracelet'  _____

3.  [telʌm]  'book'  and  [tɛlʌm]  'book'  _____

4.  [kətɑge]  'letter'  and  [kətɑge]  'paper'  _____

### PRACTICE 3.2: Minimal pairs in English

For each of the following pairs of English consonant phonemes, find two minimal pairs. Wherever possible, one pair should show one contrast in initial position and the other pair, in final position. The first pair is done for you. Don't be fooled by spelling.

1.  / p : b /  ___paste : baste___  ___rope : robe___

2.  / t : d /  _____  _____

3.  / k : g /  _____  _____

4.  / f : v /  _____  _____

5.  / s : z /  _____  _____

6.  / m : n /  _____  _____

7.  / r : l /  _____  _____

8.  / t : θ /  _____  _____

9.  / ʧ : ʤ /  _____  _____

10.  / p : f /  _____  _____

# COMPLEMENTARY DISTRIBUTION (Section 2.1, pp. 68–69)

Two sounds are in complementary distribution when they never occur in the same phonetic environment. The term *environment* refers to the phonetic context in which the sounds occur. The following exercises are designed to help you understand and determine complementary distribution.

## PRACTICE 3.3: Complementary distribution in English

1. The English phoneme /p/ has three allophones:  [ p ]  — unaspirated
   [ pʰ ]  — aspirated
   [ p̚ ]  — unreleased

The following lists of words give examples of each phonetic variant.

| [ p ] | [ pʰ ] | [ p̚ ] |
|---|---|---|
| spook | pig | collapse |
| spirit | police | apt |
| operate | appear | flipped |
| hippy | repair | ape |
| happening | | cop |
| | | clap |

On the following chart, put a check in the box if the allophone can occur in that environment. Explanations of the different environments are given below.

| | #_____ | _____# | s_____ | _____C | V́_____V | V_____V́ |
|---|---|---|---|---|---|---|
| [ p ] | | | | | | |
| [ pʰ ] | | | | | | |
| [ p̚ ] | | | | | | |

Explanations of environments:

| | | | |
|---|---|---|---|
| #_____ | word-initial position | V́_____V | between vowels (where the first vowel is stressed) |
| _____# | word-final position | V_____V́ | between vowels (where the second vowel is stressed) |
| s_____ | after [s] | | |
| _____C | before a consonant | | |

2. The English phoneme /l/ has (at least) three allophones:
   [ l ] — alveolar l
   [ ł ] — velarized l
   [ l̩ ] — syllabic l

The following lists of words give examples of each phonetic variant.

| [ l ] | [ ł ] | [ l̩ ] |
|-------|-------|--------|
| lip | swallow | paddle |
| love | silly | obstacle |
| allow | salt | twinkle |
| malign | ilk | hassle |
| slip | pull | bushel |
| slide | meal | hurdle |

On the following chart, put a check in the box if the allophone can occur in that environment. Explanations of the different environments are given below.

| | #___ | C___V | V___# | C___# | ___C | V́___V | V___V́ |
|-----|------|-------|-------|-------|------|--------|--------|
| [ l ] | | | | | | | |
| [ ł ] | | | | | | | |
| [ l̩ ] | | | | | | | |

Explanations of environments:

| | |
|---|---|
| #_____ | word-initial position |
| C_____V | between a consonant and a vowel |
| V_____# | word-final after a vowel |
| C_____# | word-final after a consonant |
| _____C | before a consonant |
| V́_____V | between vowels, where the first vowel is stressed |
| V_____V́ | between vowels, where the second vowel is stressed |

## PRACTICE 3.4: Complementary distribution in other languages

1. **Oneida:** Examine the following data from Oneida. Using the following chart, determine if the sounds [s] and [z] are or are not in complementary distribution. Note that [sh] represents [s] and [h], not [ʃ].

| | [s] | | [z] | |
|---|---|---|---|---|

[s]

| [lashet] | 'let him count' |
| [laʔsluni] | 'white men' |
| [loteswatu] | 'he's been playing' |
| [skahnehtat] | 'one pine tree' |
| [thiskate] | 'a different one' |
| [sninuhe] | 'you buy' |
| [wahsnestakeʔ] | 'you ate corn' |

[z]

| [kawenezuzeʔ] | 'long words' |
| [khaiize] | 'I'm taking it along' |
| [lazel] | 'let him drag it' |
| [tahazehteʔ] | 'he dropped it' |
| [tuzahatiteni] | 'they changed it' |
| [wezake] | 'she saw you' |

| | #___ | ___C | C___ | V___V |
|---|---|---|---|---|
| [s] | | | | |
| [z] | | | | |

2. **Oneida:** Now determine if the sounds [s] and [ʃ] are or are not in complementary distribution. Again, [sh] represents [s] and [h], not [ʃ]. Hint: Look at specific vowels or consonants in the environment.

[s]

| [lashet] | 'let him count' |
| [laʔsluni] | 'white men' |
| [loteswatu] | 'he's been playing' |
| [skahnehtat] | 'one pine tree' |
| [thiskate] | 'a different one' |
| [sninuhe] | 'you buy' |
| [wahsnestakeʔ] | 'you ate corn' |

[ʃ]

| [ʃjatuheʔ] | 'you write' |
| [tehʃjaʔk] | 'let you break' |
| [jaʔteʃjatekhahʃjahteʔ] | 'they would suddenly separate again' |

3. **Japanese:** Examine the following data from Japanese and determine if the sounds [t], [ts], and [tʃ] are or are not in complementary distribution. Set up a chart to help you. Hint: You may want to look at specific vowels in the linguistic environment.

The symbol [ts] is a single segment representing a voiceless alveolar affricate.

| 1. | [taijo:] | 'the sun' | 5. | [gaito:] | 'cloak, overcoat' |
| 2. | [tatami] | 'mat' | 6. | [koto] | 'fact' |
| 3. | [tambo] | 'rice paddy' | 7. | [tegami] | 'letter' |
| 4. | [buta] | 'pig' | 8. | [totemo] | 'very' |

| 9. | [ʧiɲɲi] | 'truly' | 14. | [iriguʧi] | 'entrance' |
| 10. | [ʧigai] | 'difference' | 15. | [tsunami] | 'tidal wave' |
| 11. | [ʧiri] | 'dust' | 16. | [tsukue] | 'desk' |
| 12. | [iʧigo] | 'strawberry' | 17. | [do:butsu] | 'animal' |
| 13. | [deguʧi] | 'exit' | 18. | [zatsuzi] | 'chores' |

# SOLVING PHONOLOGY PROBLEMS (Appendix, pp. 119–120)

The basic goal in solving a phonology problem is to determine if the sounds being examined belong to one phoneme or to separate phonemes.

**When allophones belong to separate phonemes, they are:**

1. Contrastive/distinctive
2. In unpredictable distribution
3. Easily perceived as different by native speakers
4. Not necessarily phonetically similar

**When allophones belong to the same phoneme, they are:**

1. Noncontrastive/rule-governed
2. In predictable distribution
3. Not easily perceived as different by native speakers
4. Always phonetically similar

## PROBLEM-SOLVING FLOWCHART

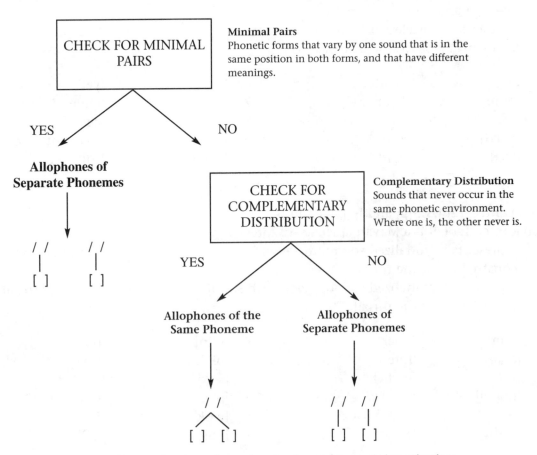

**Minimal Pairs**
Phonetic forms that vary by one sound that is in the same position in both forms, and that have different meanings.

**Complementary Distribution**
Sounds that never occur in the same phonetic environment. Where one is, the other never is.

Repeat the above for each pair of sounds you are investigating.

## PRACTICE 3.5: Distinguishing phonemes and allophones

1. **Arabic:** [h] and [ʔ]

   | | | | | |
   |---|---|---|---|---|
   | 1. | [ʔuruːb] | 'wars' | 5. | [huruːb] | 'flight' |
   | 2. | [fahm] | 'understanding' | 6. | [faʔm] | 'coal' |
   | 3. | [habba] | 'gust, squall' | 7. | [ʔabba] | 'grain, seed' |
   | 4. | [haːl] | 'cardamom' | 8. | [ʔaːl] | 'condition' |

2. **Biblical Hebrew:** [d] and [ð]
   [ɣ] represents a voiced velar fricative.
   [ʕ] represents a voiced pharyngeal fricative.
   [x] represents a voiceless velar fricative.

   | | | | | | |
   |---|---|---|---|---|---|
   | 1. | [gaðol] | 'great' | 6. | [ʕɛvɛð] | 'servant' |
   | 2. | [damim] | 'blood' | 7. | [daɣeʃ] | 'piercing' |
   | 3. | [bɛɣɛð] | 'garment' | 8. | [jəhuða] | 'Judah' |
   | 4. | [ʔaðam] | 'man' | 9. | [xɛsɛð] | 'steadfast love' |
   | 5. | [davar] | 'word' | 10. | [dawið] | 'David' |

3. **German:** [ç] and [χ]
   [ç] represents a voiceless palatal fricative.
   [χ] represents a voiceless uvular fricative.

   | | | | | | |
   |---|---|---|---|---|---|
   | 1. | [naχ] | 'to, after' | 6. | [dɔχ] | 'yet' |
   | 2. | [çemi] | 'chemistry' | 7. | [kɪrçə] | 'church' |
   | 3. | [dɪç] | 'you' | 8. | [aχaːt] | 'agate' |
   | 4. | [maχt] | 'power' | 9. | [rɛçnən] | 'to count' |
   | 5. | [rɛçt] | 'right' | 10. | [nɔχ] | 'still, yet' |

4. **Zinacantec Tzotzil:** [p] and [p'], [k] and [k']
   Zinacantec Tzotzil is a Mayan language of Mexico.
   [p'] represents a glottalized sound, made with simultaneous closure of the glottis and
      constriction of the throat.
   [k'] represents a glottalized sound, made with simultaneous closure of the glottis and
      constriction of the throat.

   | | | | | | |
   |---|---|---|---|---|---|
   | 1. | [pim] | 'thick' | 7. | [p'in] | 'pot' |
   | 2. | [bikil] | 'intestines' | 8. | [bik'it] | 'small' |
   | 3. | [ka] | 'particle' | 9. | [kok] | 'my leg' |
   | 4. | [nopol] | 'nearby' | 10. | [p'ol] | 'to multiply' |
   | 5. | [p'us] | 'hunchback' | 11. | [k'ok'] | 'fire' |
   | 6. | [k'a] | 'horse' | 12. | [pus] | 'jail' |

## PRACTICE 3.6: More practice with phonemes and allophones

The following pages contain data sets from a number of different languages (some of the data may have been regularized). Each data set contains sufficient data to make valid conclusions about the sounds under consideration. For each data set:

- state your conclusion (i.e., allophones of the same phoneme or of separate phonemes)

- provide evidence to support your conclusion

- provide a representation of the phoneme(s)

1. **English: Long and short vowels**
   [Vː] When a colon-like symbol follows a vowel, it means that the vowel is long. This means that we take a longer time saying the vowel; do not confuse this use of the term *long vowel* with what you may have learned in elementary school (where the term referred to a vowel that sounds like the name of the letter).

   | | | | | | | |
   |---|---|---|---|---|---|---|
   | 1. | [gɪft] | 'gift' | 7. | [hʌːg] | 'hug' |
   | 2. | [rɑːbd] | 'robbed' | 8. | [nowt] | 'note' |
   | 3. | [lʌk] | 'luck' | 9. | [gɪːv] | 'give' |
   | 4. | [moːwd] | 'mowed' | 10. | [sliːz] | 'sleaze' |
   | 5. | [slæpt] | 'slapped' | 11. | [pɑt] | 'pot' |
   | 6. | [mejs] | 'mace' | 12. | [kræːb] | 'crab' |

   You could treat each vowel individually. However, it will be more efficient if you treat long vowels as a class. Assume that English has either short and corresponding long vowels as separate phonemes, or short and corresponding long vowels as allophones of the same phonemes.

2. **Korean:** [l] and [ř]
   [ř] represents a flapped [r].
   [ʉ] represents a high central rounded vowel.

   | | | | | | | |
   |---|---|---|---|---|---|---|
   | 1. | [kal] | 'dog' | 11. | [silkwa] | 'fruit' |
   | 2. | [kenel] | 'shade' | 12. | [mul] | 'water' |
   | 3. | [iřumi] | 'name' | 13. | [seul] | 'Seoul' |
   | 4. | [kiři] | 'road' | 14. | [kəřiřo] | 'to the street' |
   | 5. | [juŋuʧʉm] | 'receipt' | 15. | [sařam] | 'person' |
   | 6. | [pal] | 'leg' | 16. | [tatʉl] | 'all of them' |
   | 7. | [ilkop] | 'seven' | 17. | [vəřʉm] | 'summer' |
   | 8. | [ipalsa] | 'barber' | | | |
   | 9. | [uři] | 'we' | | | |
   | 10. | [onelppam] | 'tonight' | | | |

3. **Inuktitut:** [u] and [a]
   [q] represents a voiceless uvular stop.

   | | | | | | | |
   |---|---|---|---|---|---|---|
   | 1. | [iglumut] | 'to a house' | | 6. | [aniguvit] | 'if you leave' |
   | 2. | [ukiaq] | 'late fall' | | 7. | [ini] | 'place, spot' |
   | 3. | [iglu] | '(snow)house' | | 8. | [ukiuq] | 'winter' |
   | 4. | [aiviq] | 'walrus' | | 9. | [ani] | 'female's brother' |
   | 5. | [pinna] | 'that one up there' | | 10. | [anigavit] | 'because you leave' |

4. **English:** [g], [gʲ] and [gʷ]
   [gʲ] represents a fronted [g], made with the back of the tongue at or near the hard palate.
   [gʷ] represents a rounded [g], made with simultaneous lip rounding.

   | | | | | | | |
   |---|---|---|---|---|---|---|
   | 1. | [gɔn] | 'gone' | | 7. | [gʲik] | 'geek' |
   | 2. | [gʷufi] | 'goofy' | | 8. | [igər] | 'eager' |
   | 3. | [gli] | 'glee' | | 9. | [gejm] | 'game' |
   | 4. | [slʌg] | 'slug' | | 10. | [gowfər] | 'gopher' |
   | 5. | [grin] | 'green' | | 11. | [gædʒət] | 'gadget' |
   | 6. | [rægʷu] | 'Ragu' | | 12. | [gʲis] | 'geese' |

5. **Yakut:** [i], [ɨ], [y] and [u]
   Yakut is a Turkic language of northeastern Siberia.
   [ɨ] represents a high central unrounded vowel.
   [y] represents a high front rounded vowel.

   For these sounds to be allophones of separate phonemes, you must find a minimal pair for:

   - [i] and [ɨ]
   - [i] and [y]
   - [i] and [u]
   - [ɨ] and [y]
   - [ɨ] and [u]
   - [y] and [u]

   You may use the same data item in more than one pair.

   | | | | | | | |
   |---|---|---|---|---|---|---|
   | 1. | [bit] | 'mark' | | 8. | [ɨt] | 'shoot' |
   | 2. | [il] | 'peace' | | 9. | [tys] | 'descend' |
   | 3. | [sil] | 'saliva' | | 10. | [byt] | 'end' |
   | 4. | [kir] | 'nibble' | | 11. | [sur] | 'gray' |
   | 5. | [tɨs] | 'paw' | | 12. | [kur] | 'belt' |
   | 6. | [ɨk] | 'wring' | | 13. | [uk] | 'insert' |
   | 7. | [sɨl] | 'year' | | 14. | [tus] | 'directly' |

# NEAR-MINIMAL PAIRS AND FREE VARIATION
(Section 2.2, pp. 69–71)

**Near-Minimal Pairs:**   Pairs that have segments in nearly identical phonetic environments. They can also be used to establish that sounds contrast.
e.g., Hindi [bara] 'large' and [ḅari] 'heavy'

**Free Variation:**   Sounds that occur in identical phonetic environments, but that do not make a meaning difference.
e.g., English [stɑpʔ] or [stɑp˺]

## PRACTICE 3.7: Near-minimal pairs and free variation

For each of the following data sets, determine whether the sounds are allophones of separate phonemes, allophones of the same phoneme, or in free variation.

1. **Yuchi:** [t] and [tʰ]
   Yuchi is a Native American language originally spoken in the Southeast, especially in Georgia, and preserved until the late twentieth century in Oklahoma.
   A tilde over a vowel represents a nasalized vowel.

   | | | | | | |
   |---|---|---|---|---|---|
   | 1. | [geta] | 'hold on to' | 8. | [gotʰi] | 'beg' |
   | 2. | [dotũ] | 'I will suck' | 9. | [histaʔẽ] | 'flat' |
   | 3. | [getjoʔo] | 'belch' | 10. | [hõsatʰæ] | 'his heart' |
   | 4. | [setʰwa] | 'she kills' | 11. | [gotʰa] | 'pick' |
   | 5. | [tʰoti] | 'brown hair' | 12. | [ti] | 'rock' |
   | 6. | [tedãʃu] | 'reins' | 13. | [ʃta] | 'snow' |
   | 7. | [gotʰo] | 'head' | 14. | [hõsatʰẽ] | 'he shaves' |

2. **Spanish:** [b] and [β]
   [β] is a voiced bilabial fricative.

   | | | | | | |
   |---|---|---|---|---|---|
   | 1. | [boka] | 'mouth' | 6. | [bala] | 'ball' |
   | 2. | [aβana] | 'Havana' | 7. | [kuβa] | 'Cuba' |
   | 3. | [uβa] | 'grape' | 8. | [nuβe] | 'cloud' |
   | 4. | [bonito] | 'pretty' | 9. | [ombre] | 'man' |
   | 5. | [boða] | 'wedding' | 10. | [taβako] | 'tobacco' |

# PHONETIC AND PHONEMIC TRANSCRIPTION
(Section 3, pp. 76–78)

As we learned in the last chapter, phonetic transcription is a representation of normal, everyday speech. That is, it is a representation of pronunciation. Phonetic transcription is always indicated with [ ] brackets. In this chapter, we have been learning about phonemes, which represent the knowledge a native speaker has about how sounds pattern in his or her language. We can represent this knowledge using phonemic transcription. Phonemic transcription, as the name suggests, contains the phonemes of the language and is always indicated with / / slashes.

To understand the difference between phonetic and phonemic transcription, let's reconsider the English problem concerning allophones of /g/ on p. 42. Remember that in English, [g], [gʷ], and [gʲ] are allophones of the same phoneme, with [gʲ] occurring before front vowels, [gʷ] occurring before back vowels, and [g] occurring elsewhere. Given this information, we can convert English phonetic transcription into English phonemic transcription:

| Phonetic | Phonemic | |
|---|---|---|
| [gʷufi] | /gufi/ | 'goofy' |
| [gʲik] | /gik/ | 'geek' |
| [slʌg] | /slʌg/ | 'slug' |

Notice that in the phonemic transcription, only the phoneme /g/ has been used, while in the phonetic transcription, the allophones [gʲ] and [gʷ] have both been used, along with [g]. Also notice that in the phonetic transcription, [gʲ] occurs only before front vowels, and [gʷ] occurs only before back vowels, while in phonemic transcription, /g/ occurs in all environments.

**Remember:** The main difference between phonetic and phonemic transcription is that

- phonetic transcription includes both predictable and unpredictable phonetic information, while

- phonemic transcription includes only the unpredictable information. Anything that is predictable is excluded.

## PRACTICE 3.8: Phonemic transcription

To practice phonemic transcription, return to the phonology problems in Practice 3.6 and 3.7, and wherever allophones of the same phoneme were found, convert the first few words in the data set from the phonetic transcription provided into phonemic transcription.

# SYLLABLES (Section 4, pp. 79–91)

A syllable is a unit of representation consisting of one or more segments. There are four pieces of information crucial to understanding syllables, their structure, and their role in phonology. Make sure you know them.

- **Syllables** (Section 4.1, pp. 79–80). A syllable (σ) consists of three parts: an obligatory nucleus (N), an optional onset (O), and an optional coda (Co). Onsets are segments that occur before the nucleus, while codas are segments occurring after the nucleus. The nucleus and the coda form the rhyme (R) of the syllable.

- **Phonotactics** (Sections 4.2–4.3, pp. 80–82). Phonotactics is the set of constraints on which segments can occur together. For example, in English, [pl] is an acceptable onset, as in the word *please*, but [tl] is not an acceptable onset: words in English do not begin with this combination of sounds. Phonotactics can vary from language to language.

- **Accidental and systematic gaps** (Section 4.3, pp. 82–83). Not all combinations of sounds are found in the words of a language. Accidental gaps refer to nonoccurring but possible forms, while systematic gaps refer to the exclusion of certain sequences. For example, the lack of words beginning with [ft] in English is not accidental but systematic, as such a sequence is unacceptable to speakers of the language. In contrast, that English does not have a word such as *frip* is accidental, since many existing words begin with [fr] (e.g., *frog*).

- **Syllable representations** (Section 4.4, pp. 83–87). When diagrammed, syllables are represented above the segments comprising them. In this sense, they are suprasegmental units. There are three, and sometimes four, steps to putting together a representation of a syllable. These are illustrated below for the word *template*.

| | | |
|---|---|---|
| **First:** | Assign the nucleus, the rhyme, and the syllable node. Vowels (including diphthongs) and syllabic consonants may occupy the nucleus position. Diphthongs are often diagrammed as a branching nucleus. | σ   σ<br>\|    \|<br>R    R<br>\|    \|<br>N    N<br>\|    ∧<br>tʰ ε m pl ej t |

| | | |
|---|---|---|
| **Second:** | Assign the onset. These are the segments to the left of the nucleus. Segments assigned to the onset are usually the largest sequence of sounds that can occur at the beginning of a word within a language. | σ   σ<br>∧   ∧<br>/R   /R<br>/ \|  / \|<br>O N  O N<br>\| \|  ∧ ∧<br>tʰ ε m pl ej t |

| | | |
|---|---|---|
| **Third:** | Assign the coda. These are the segments to the right of the nucleus, which have not yet been syllabified into an onset.<br><br>*Open syllables* have no coda, while *closed syllables* have a coda. | 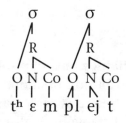 |

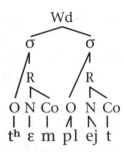

**Fourth:** As you can see from the representation being constructed, words can consist of a number of syllables. The last step in constructing syllabic representations simply involves combining syllables into words.

This step, however, is frequently omitted.

## PRACTICE 3.9: Syllables in English

Construct a syllable representation for each of the following English words. Remember to put them into phonetic transcription first. Underline all open syllables.

| | | |
|---|---|---|
| 1. garden | 4. twinkle | 7. lovely |
| 2. downtown | 5. understand | 8. satisfy |
| 3. banana | 6. beauty | 9. property |

---

### REMINDER

Syllable structure is constructed above the segments, NOT below.

---

**Variation in Syllable Structure:** Syllable structure can vary from language to language, yet the process for building syllable representation, as outlined above, can still be used.

## PRACTICE 3.10: Syllable structure in other languages

In the following language data, all syllables have the structure CV(C). This means that all syllables begin with an onset, but do not have to have a coda. That is, codas are optional. Construct syllable representations for the following words. The data are already in phonetic transcription.

1.                              2.                              3.

[z i ʧ n o]           [t a g k u]           [s e d n a k u]
'chair'                   'shell'                   'sofa'

**Syllables and Phonology:** Syllables are often relevant to stating generalizations about the distribution of allophones. For example, English aspirated stops are found at the beginning of stressed syllables, and unaspirated stops are found elsewhere. Similarly, phonetic length is predictable in English: long vowels are found before voiced coda consonants.

**PRACTICE 3.11**: Syllables and phonology

The following data are from the same language as above. In this language, stress is predictable and is marked by a [ ´ ] over a vowel. By making reference to syllable structure, determine where stress occurs.

Hint: You might want to first syllabify some of the words using the syllabification procedure from above.

| | | | | | |
|---|---|---|---|---|---|
| 1. | [fémba] | 'foot' | 8. | [póbzuʤi] | 'lizard' |
| 2. | [hagút] | 'month' | 9. | [gaʧótfobi] | 'knee' |
| 3. | [fezók] | 'music' | 10. | [talagubiták] | 'cowboy' |
| 4. | [waláp] | 'mole' | 11. | [páfzuliha] | 'thin' |
| 5. | [supóspa] | 'gravy' | 12. | [kéllaboga] | 'arm' |
| 6. | [tugábʧo] | 'stone' | | | |
| 7. | [jumajumáp] | 'armadillo with cherry sauce' | | | |

# FEATURES (Sections 5.1–5.2, pp. 91–103)

Features represent individual phonetic properties. For example, the feature [voice] represents the two different glottal states: voiced and voiceless. A "plus" value indicates that a feature is present, while a "minus" value indicates that a feature is absent. For example, voiced sounds are [+voice] while voiceless sounds are [–voice]. Features are divided into four groups as follows:

- Major class features
  [+/–consonantal], [+/–syllabic], [+/–sonorant]

- Manner features
  [+/–continuant], [+/–delayed release (DR)], [+/–nasal], [+/–lateral]

- Laryngeal features
  [+/–voice], [+/–spread glottis (SG)], [+/–constricted glottis (CG)]

- Place features
  [LABIAL], [+/–round]
  [CORONAL], [+/–anterior], [+/–strident]
  [DORSAL], [+/–high], [+/–low], [+/–back], [+/–tense], [+/–reduced]

Place features work in a slightly different way than do the major class, manner, and laryngeal features. While all of the major class, manner, and laryngeal features have both plus and minus specifications, the three place features [LABIAL], [CORONAL], and [DORSAL] have no specifications. These features are used to represent the articulator that is active in the articulation. The remaining place features do have plus and minus specifications, and are used to represent place of articulation features specific to the active articulator. For example, labial sounds can be either [+round] or [–round]; coronal sounds can be either [+anterior] or [–anterior]; and dorsal sounds can be either [+high] or [–high].

**Features are used:**

- **To represent sounds.** Features represent phonetic properties, and sounds are simply a number of phonetic properties executed simultaneously. Sounds, therefore, are composed of features. Features can be used to describe both vowels and consonants. See pages 100–103 in the text for how to determine the features making up a sound, as well as pages 103–104 for feature charts of English vowels and consonants.

- **To capture natural classes.** Natural classes are groups of sounds that share a feature or features, or which pattern together in a sound system. For example, voiceless stops can be considered a natural class, as can rounded vowels.

- **To understand the nature of allophonic variation.** For example, voiceless sounds often change and become voiced when near other voiced sounds. This can be captured with a single feature.

## PRACTICE 3.12: Features

1. State the feature that distinguishes each of the following pairs of sounds. (There may be more than one correct answer.) The first one is done for you.

    a. [θ] / [ð]  _____[+/– voice]_____

    b. [p] / [f]  _____

    c. [s] / [θ]  _____

    d. [b] / [m]  _____

    e. [ʧ] / [ʃ]  _____

2. Each of the following sets contains three sounds that belong to the same natural class. Add one other segment to each set, making sure that the natural class is preserved. Indicate the feature (including its value) that distinguishes the natural class. The first one is done for you.

| | Segment Added | Distinctive Feature |
|---|---|---|
| a. [l̩ ə n̩] | [ o ] | [+ syllabic] |
| b. [θ s f] | [  ] | _____ |
| c. [p m k] | [  ] | _____ |
| d. [j r n] | [  ] | _____ |

3.  Name the natural class that each of the following phonetic matrices describes.

a.
$$\begin{bmatrix} -\text{consonantal} \\ -\text{syllabic} \end{bmatrix}$$

b.
$$\begin{bmatrix} +\text{consonantal} \\ -\text{syllabic} \\ -\text{sonorant} \\ +\text{continuant} \\ +\text{voice} \end{bmatrix}$$

4.  In each of the following sets, all the sounds except one constitute a natural class. Draw a circle around the sound that does not belong, and state the feature that the remaining sounds share.

a. [ t  g  v  ʤ ]  _____

b. [ j  m  ʒ  w ]  _____

c. [ m  g  d  r ]  _____

d. [ ʧ  m  t  ŋ ]  _____

5.  In each of the following consonant systems, some segments are boxed. Determine if the boxed segments constitute a natural class. If they do, state the feature(s) that make them a

a.

```
p   t   ┌─────┐
        │  k  │
f   s   │     │
m   n   │  ŋ  │
    l   │     │
w       │  j  │
        └─────┘
```

b.

```
p   ┌───┐       k   ʔ
    │ t │
f   │ s ʃ │         h
    │ r │
    └───┘
```

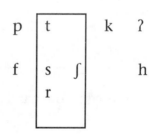

c.

```
p   t   k
v   z
┌───────────┐
│ m   n     │
│     l̩     │
│       i  u│
│         ɑ │
└───────────┘
```

d.

```
p   t   k
┌───────────┐
│ b   d   g │
└───────────┘
┌───────────┐
│ m   n   ŋ │
│     l     │
└───────────┘
```

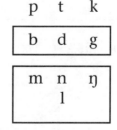

natural class.

6.  For each of the following groups of sounds, provide a feature matrix for features shared by the group. Then tell which feature or features distinguish individual sounds in the group from each other.

a. [ð θ f v]                    c. [u o]

b. [g ʤ]                        d. [i ɪ e ɛ æ]

# RULES AND STATEMENTS (Section 6.3, pp. 108–112)

Allophones of the same phoneme represent a predictable sound change. Because these sounds are predictable, a rule and a statement can be put together capturing their distribution. Rules and statements convey the same information, the difference being that rules use phonological notation, while statements use general articulatory descriptions.

Rules and statements have three parts:

1.  the phoneme
2.  the allophone (what the change is)
3.  the phonetic environment (where the change occurs)

## PRACTICE 3.13: Rules and statements

1.  Convert these statements into rules. Watch out for natural classes.

    a.  Voiced oral stops become voiceless at the beginning of words.

    _____

    b.  Alveopalatal affricates become fricatives between vowels.

    _____

    c.  Vowels become nasalized before nasals.

    _____

    d.  Schwa is deleted word-finally.

    _____

    e.  A schwa is inserted between a voiceless bilabial stop and a voiced lateral liquid.

    _____

2.  Convert the following rules into statements.

a.   t   $\longrightarrow$   tˀ   /   ʔ_____

b.   $\begin{Bmatrix} f \\ s \\ \theta \\ \int \end{Bmatrix}$   $\longrightarrow$   $\begin{Bmatrix} v \\ z \\ ð \\ ʒ \end{Bmatrix}$   /   V_____V

c.   $\begin{Bmatrix} i \\ e \end{Bmatrix}$   $\longrightarrow$   $\begin{Bmatrix} ɪ \\ ɛ \end{Bmatrix}$   /   _____#

d.   $\begin{Bmatrix} p \\ t \\ k \end{Bmatrix}$   $\longrightarrow$   $\begin{Bmatrix} p^h \\ t^h \\ k^h \end{Bmatrix}$   /   #_____V́

3.  Go back over the rules given (not the statements you constructed) in exercise 2 and formulate them using feature matrices rather than phonetic symbols. Do the same for the rules you constructed (not the statements given) in exercise 1.

## PRACTICE 3.14: Discovering rules

For each of the following problems, decide what, if any, phonological process is in operation. If there is no process and the phonemes are in free variation, give evidence for your answer. If there is a phonological process involved, write a rule.

1. **Polish: Voiced and voiceless stops**
   Voiced and voiceless stops are separate phonemes in Polish.

   | | | | | | |
   |---|---|---|---|---|---|
   | 1. | [klup] | 'club' | 7. | [klubi] | 'clubs' |
   | 2. | [trup] | 'corpse' | 8. | [trupi] | 'corpses' |
   | 3. | [trut] | 'labor' | 9. | [trudi] | 'labors' |
   | 4. | [kot] | 'cat' | 10. | [koti] | 'cats' |
   | 5. | [wuk] | 'lye' | 11. | [wugi] | 'lyes' |
   | 6. | [sok] | 'juice' | 12. | [soki] | 'juices' |

2. **South Midland and Southern American English: [ɪ] and [ɛ]**
   In some areas of the U.S., the phonemes [ɪ] and [ɛ] have merged in certain words. Is this a case of free variation, or is it predictable? If you think it is free variation, give evidence for your answer. If you think it is predictable, write a rule.

   | | | | | | |
   |---|---|---|---|---|---|
   | 1. | [bɪn] | 'Ben' | 7. | [sɪt] | 'sit' |
   | 2. | [pʰɪn] | 'pin' | 8. | [sɪnt] | 'cent' |
   | 3. | [bɛt] | 'bet' | 9. | [rɛk] | 'wreck' |
   | 4. | [bɪt] | 'bit' | 10. | [hɪm] | 'hem' |
   | 5. | [pʰɪn] | 'pen' | 11. | [hɛlow] | 'hello' |
   | 6. | [sɛt] | 'set' | 12. | [hɪm] | 'hymn' |

## DERIVATIONS (Sections 6.1–6.2, pp. 107–109)

Derivations are a representation of how phonemes and allophones are related. Phonetic forms are derived from phonemic forms by applying rules. There are three parts to a derivation. These parts are very similar to the components of a phonological rule.

- **Underlying representation (UR).** The underlying representation is a representation of native speaker knowledge and therefore is always in phonemic transcription.

- **Rules.** Remember that phonemes and allophones are linked by a rule. The rule applies to change the phoneme into the allophone. This, of course, only occurs when the structural description (environment) specified in the rule is found in the underlying representation.

- **Phonetic representation (PR).** The phonetic representation is also called the surface representation. It is the output of the application of a rule. Since the surface representation always represents pronunciation, it is in phonetic transcription.

Recall from discussions that, in English, liquids become voiceless after a voiceless stop at the beginning of a syllable. This is an example of devoicing and can be captured with a rule such as:

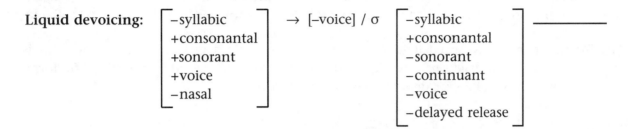

Liquid devoicing: $\begin{bmatrix} -\text{syllabic} \\ +\text{consonantal} \\ +\text{sonorant} \\ +\text{voice} \\ -\text{nasal} \end{bmatrix} \rightarrow [-\text{voice}] / \sigma \begin{bmatrix} -\text{syllabic} \\ +\text{consonantal} \\ -\text{sonorant} \\ -\text{continuant} \\ -\text{voice} \\ -\text{delayed release} \end{bmatrix} \underline{\hspace{2cm}}$

The first feature matrix captures the class of liquids. The second part of the rule captures the change in voicing that occurs. The third part of the rule captures that the rule only applies after a voiceless stop at the beginning of a syllable. Recall that σ is used to indicate a syllable.

The following derivation captures the relationship between English voiced and voiceless liquids as shown by the above rule.

| UR | # pliz # | 'please' | # læf # | 'laugh' |
|---|---|---|---|---|
| Liquid devoicing | # pl̥iz # | | _____ | |
| PR | [ pl̥iz ] | | [ læf ] | |

In the word *please,* liquid devoicing applies because [l] occurs after a voiceless consonant (i.e., [p]). The structural description of the rule has been met. Notice that after the rule has applied, [l] has become voiceless (i.e., [l̥]). The rule does not apply to the word *laugh,* since the structural description necessary for the rule to apply was not met: [l] occurs at the beginning of the word and not after a voiceless consonant. The phonetic form, therefore, remains the same as the underlying form.

## RULE ORDERING (Section 6.2, pp. 108–109)

More than one rule can apply during the derivation of a particular form. Sometimes the order in which rules apply is crucial to deriving the appropriate phonetic form. That is, one rule must apply before another. Such a relationship is called *feeding:* the application of one rule creates the environment for the second. A good example of this relationship involves the rule of liquid devoicing (from p. 58) and the rule of schwa deletion presented below.

Schwa deletion: $[ə] \rightarrow Ø / C_Ø \underline{\hspace{1.5cm}} \sigma \; C_Ø \; \underset{[+\text{stress}]}{V}$

The first and second parts of the rule refer to the deletion of schwa. The third part of the rule captures that this occurs only when schwa is in an open syllable followed by a stressed syllable. The first $C_\emptyset$ represents any number of successive onset consonants from zero up that may occur before schwa. $\sigma$ represents the syllable boundary, and the second $C_\emptyset$ again represents any onset consonants that may occur before the stressed vowel of the next syllable.

**The Incorrect Order:** Schwa deletion must apply before liquid devoicing. If liquid devoicing is applied before schwa deletion, then liquids incorrectly remain voiced in the phonetic form. This is shown in the following derivation of the word *police*.

| UR | # pəlís #        'police' |
| --- | --- |
| Liquid devoicing | ——— |
| Schwa deletion | # plís # |
| PR | [ plís ] |

(**Note:** It is assumed that stress placement has already occurred. Normally, stress would not be present in the underlying form because it is predictable in English, and therefore would be applied using a stress rule.)

**The Correct Order:** Since liquids in English are produced without voice following a voiceless stop, schwa deletion must occur first so that in the resulting output, liquids occur after voiceless stops, creating the necessary environment for liquid devoicing to apply.

| UR | # pəlís #        'police' |
| --- | --- |
| Schwa deletion | # plís # |
| Liquid devoicing | # plís # |
| PR | [ plis ] |

As shown in the above derivation, the phonetic form now contains, as it should in English, a voiceless liquid.

## PRACTICE 3.15: Rules and derivations

For each data set:

- Determine if the sounds are allophones of the same phoneme or allophones of separate phonemes. If they are allophones of the same phoneme, determine whether they are in complementary distribution or in free variation. Remember to provide evidence in support of your conclusion along with a representation of the phoneme(s).

- For all allophones of the same phoneme, provide a rule and a statement. Wherever possible, try to write one rule and statement for all the sounds you have investigated. Hint: Watch out for natural classes.

- For all allophones of the same phoneme involving natural classes, write a rule using feature notation.

- For all allophones of the same phoneme, identify the articulatory process at work.

- Provide derivations as indicated.


1. **Tamil:** [p] and [b], [k] and [g], [ʈ] and [ɖ], [t̪] and [d̪]
   [ʈ], [ɖ] are retroflex.
   [ ̪ ] means that a sound is dental.
   [ ɨ ] represents a high central unrounded vowel

   Remember:  When looking for complementary distribution, you must record the
             immediate surrounding phonetic environment around each occurrence
             of a sound.

   | | | | |
   |---|---|---|---|
   | 1. [pal] | 'tooth' | 11. [id̪ɨ] | 'this' |
   | 2. [abayam] | 'refuge' | 12. [aɖɨ] | 'that' |
   | 3. [kappal] | 'ship' | 13. [kat̪t̪i] | 'knife' |
   | 4. [saabam] | 'curse' | 14. [kuɖi] | 'jump' |
   | 5. [kaakkaaj] | 'crow' | 15. [patti] | 'ten' |
   | 6. [mugil] | 'cloud' | 16. [paaɖam] | 'foot' |
   | 7. [t̪ugil] | 'veil' | 17. [iɖam] | 'place' |
   | 8. [t̪at̪t̪i] | 'plate' | 18. [kaat̪paaɖi] | 'name of a town' |
   | 9. [padɨ] | 'lie down' | 19. [pat̪t̪ɨ] | 'silk' |
   | 10. [t̪uukkɨ] | 'carry' | | |

   - Provide a derivation for nos. 3, 6, and 14.

2. **Gascon:** [b] and [β],  [d] and [ð],  [g] and [ɣ]
Hint: Think about what process you would expect given pairs of stops and fricatives.
[ɣ] represents a voiced velar fricative.

| | | | | |
|---|---|---|---|---|
| 1. [brẽn] | 'endanger' | 10. [ʒuɣɛt] | 'he played' |
| 2. [dilys] | 'Monday' | 11. [krãmbo] | 'room' |
| 3. [taldepãn] | 'leftover bread' | 12. [eʃaðo] | 'hoe' |
| 4. [ʃiβaw] | 'horse' | 13. [gat] | 'cat' |
| 5. [pũnde] | 'to lay eggs' | 14. [aβe] | 'to have' |
| 6. [agro] | 'sour' | 15. [biɣar] | 'mosquito' |
| 7. [puðe] | 'to be able' | 16. [ũmbro] | 'shadow' |
| 8. [riɣut] | 'he laughed' | 17. [dudze] | 'twelve' |
| 9. [noβi] | 'husband' | 18. [lũŋg] | 'long' |

- Examine the Gascon data again, paying attention to the oral and nasal vowels. Can you make any conclusions about nasalized vowels in this language? Write one statement involving classes of sounds, describing their behavior.

- Provide derivations for nos. 3, 9, 12, and 16. Do your rules need to be ordered? Why or why not?

---

### REMINDER

To solve a phonology problem, you must have a firm grasp on minimal pairs, near-minimal pairs, and complementary distribution. If you don't, then you need to get some help.

---

## REVIEW EXERCISE

Determine: (1) whether the sounds under consideration are allophones of the same phoneme or are separate phonemes, and (2) whether they are in free variation. Provide evidence to support your conclusion. If the sounds are allophones of the same phoneme, state whether they are in free variation or in complementary distribution. If they are in free variation, provide evidence for your conclusion. If they are in complementary distribution, provide a phonological rule.

1. **Passamaquoddy:** [p] and [b]
Passamaquoddy (Maliseet) is a Native American language spoken in Maine and Canada.

| | | | | |
|---|---|---|---|---|
| 1. [aptʃədʒ] | 'good-bye' | 5. [əptan] | 'coat' |
| 2. [wiphun] | 'feather' | 6. [əbu] | 'he sits' |
| 3. [aptʃ] | 'again' | 7. [wibid] | 'his tooth' |
| 4. [zipsiz] | 'bird' | 8. [wabeju] | 'white' |

2. **Kpelle: Nasalized and oral vowels**
   Kpelle is a tone language spoken in Liberia and Sierra Leone. Tones have been omitted in the data here. A tilde [˜] over a vowel indicates that it is nasalized.

| | | | | | |
|---|---|---|---|---|---|
| 1. | [sĩi] | 'spider' | 6. | [kpẽla] | 'water chevrotain'* |
| 2. | [nsũa] | 'my nose' | 7. | [põja] | 'a design, mark' |
| 3. | [nũui] | 'the person' | 8. | [mẽla] | 'its horn' |
| 4. | [mela] | 'split it' | 9. | [ntɛɛ] | 'send me' |
| 5. | [ntĩa] | 'my taboo' | 10. | [nsoŋ] | 'catch me' |

   \* A water chevrotain is a hornless ruminant, also called a mouse deer.

3. **Hausa: [r] and [ɽ]**
   Hausa is a language spoken in northern Nigeria. Tones are not shown here.
   [r] represents a trill.
   [ɽ] represents a retroflex flap.
   [ɓ] represents a voiced bilabial implosive, in which the larynx moves downward, sucking air in.

| | | | | | |
|---|---|---|---|---|---|
| 1. | [ʃaːɽaː] | 'sweeping' | 6. | [rubuːtuː] | 'writing' |
| 2. | [ʃahararreː] | 'famous' | 7. | [bargoː] | 'blanket' |
| 3. | [ɓaɽgoː] | 'marrow' | 8. | [ʃaːɽaɽɽeː] | 'swept' |
| 4. | [ɽuɓeːwaː] | 'rotting' | 9. | [kʷoːɽaː] | 'ringworm' |
| 5. | [baraː] | 'begging' | 10. | [gʷoːro] | 'kola nut' |

4. **Bemba: [s] and [ʃ]**
   Bemba is a Bantu language spoken in Zambia and elsewhere in East Africa.
   Tones are not shown here.

| | | | | | |
|---|---|---|---|---|---|
| 1. | [ukuʃika] | 'to be deep' | 8. | [insa] | 'clock, hour' |
| 2. | [amakalaʃi] | 'glasses' | 9. | [isabi] | 'fish' |
| 3. | [umuʃikaːle] | 'soldier' | 10. | [fuseːke] | 'go away!' |
| 4. | [ameːnʃi] | 'water' | 11. | [ukusela] | 'to move' |
| 5. | [umwaːnakaʃi] | 'woman' | 12. | [akasuba] | 'sun' |
| 6. | [insoːkoʃi] | 'socks' | 13. | [soma] | 'read!' |
| 7. | [nʃi] | 'what' | 14. | [pasoːpo] | 'beware!' |

5. **Syrian Arabic:** [s] and [sˤ], [z] and [zˤ]
   [sˤ] and [zˤ]  are pharyngealized; they are formed with a secondary articulation involving a constriction in the pharynx.

| | | | | |
|---|---|---|---|---|
| 1. | [nəsˤsˤ] | 'half' | 9. [sˤeːf] | 'summer' |
| 2. | [buːzˤa] | 'ice cream' | 10. [nəsər] | 'eagle' |
| 3. | [sˤadˤme] | 'shock' | 11. [naːs] | 'people' |
| 4. | [seːf] | 'sword' | 12. [wəsˤex] | 'dirty' |
| 5. | [nizˤaːm] | 'discipline' | 13. [sahəl] | 'easy' |
| 6. | [zahər] | 'flower' | 14. [buːz] | 'muzzle' |
| 7. | [sˤəhər] | 'sister's husband' | 15. [ħəzer] | 'careful' |
| 8. | [fazˤzˤ] | 'crude' | 16. [zˤaːher] | 'apparent' |

6. **Malay:** [t] and [tʲ]
   [ʲ] represents a sound that has been palatalized.

| | | | | |
|---|---|---|---|---|
| 1. | [mata] | 'eye' | 8. [ʧantik] | 'beautiful' |
| 2. | [tʲarek] | 'rip' | 9. [batʲa] | 'steel' |
| 3. | [ʧampah] | 'tasteless' | 10. [təgoh] | 'firm' |
| 4. | [kətil] | 'pinch' | 11. [ʧomel] | 'cute' |
| 5. | [ʧinta] | 'love' | 12. [tuma] | 'louse' |
| 6. | [ketʲut] | 'shriveled' | 13. [laut] | 'sea' |
| 7. | [tarek] | 'pull' | 14. [tʲampah] | 'tasteless' |

Look at the data again and examine [ʧ] and [tʲ]. Are these separate phonemes, allophones in complementary distribution, or allophones in free variation? Give evidence to support your answer.

 **RECAP**

Make sure you know how to do the following. (See also the Key Terms on pp. 117–118 of the main text.)

- define phonemes and allophones
- spot minimal and near-minimal pairs
- find free variation
- determine complementary distribution
- construct representations of phonemes
- construct syllable representations
- spot open and closed syllables
- identify consonantal and vowel features
- put together feature matrices
- put together rules and statements
- put together rules using feature notation
- construct derivations
- solve phonology problems

# QUESTIONS? PROBLEMS?

# four

# MORPHOLOGY: THE ANALYSIS OF WORD STRUCTURE

Morphology is the study of words and how they are formed and interpreted. Following are some of the important topics and concepts covered in this chapter. Make sure you are familiar with them.

| | |
|---|---|
| Morphological terminology | Form vs. function |
| Identifying morphemes | Compounding |
| Identifying lexical categories | Other morphological processes |
| Constructing word trees | Other word-formation processes |
| Inflection | Morphology problems |
| Derivation | Morphophonemics |

## MORPHOLOGICAL TERMINOLOGY

The following terms are crucial to understanding morphology. You should know them. (Remember also to review the Key Terms at the end of Chapter 4 in the main text.)

- word
- simple word
- complex word

- morpheme
- free morpheme
- bound morpheme (affix)

- allomorphs

- root
- base
- stem

- prefix
- suffix
- infix

# IDENTIFYING MORPHEMES (Section 1.1, pp. 133–135)

Morphemes are the building blocks of words. A word may contain only one morpheme, making it a simple word, or a word may contain more than one morpheme, making it a complex word. Below are some hints for determining the number of morphemes that a word contains.

- A morpheme can carry information about meaning or function. For example, the word *haunt* cannot be divided into the morphemes *h* and *aunt*, since only *aunt* has meaning. However, the word *bats* has two morphemes, since both *bat* and *-s* have meaning. The *-s*, of course, means that there is more than one.

- The meanings of individual morphemes should contribute to the overall meaning of the word. For example, *pumpkin* cannot be divided into *pump* and *kin*, since the meaning of *pumpkin* has nothing to do with the meaning of either *pump* or *kin*.

- A morpheme is not the same as a syllable. Morphemes do not have to be a syllable, or morphemes can consist of one or more syllables. For example, the morpheme *treat* has one syllable, the morpheme *dracula* has three syllables, but the morpheme *-s* (meaning 'plural') is not a syllable.

- Often during word formation, changes in pronunciation and/or spelling occur. These do not affect a morpheme's status as a morpheme. For example, when *-y* is attached to the word *scare*, it becomes *scary*, and when *-er* is attached to *scary*, it becomes *scarier*. The root, however, is still *scare*, not *scar*.

## PRACTICE 4.1: Identifying morphemes

Identify the number of morphemes in each of the following words.

1. desert  _____

2. memory _____

3. format  _____

4. flowchart _____

5. bug  _____

6. debug  _____

7. supply  _____

8. supplies  _____

9. supplier  _____

10. faster  _____

11. power  _____

12. processor  _____

## FREE AND BOUND MORPHEMES (Section 1.1, pp. 133–135)

A **free morpheme** can stand on its own as a word (e.g., *scare, treat, dracula*). A **bound morpheme** must be attached to another element and cannot be a word by itself (e.g., scar*y*, treat-*ed*, pumpkin*s*).

### PRACTICE 4.2: Free and bound morphemes

For each of the following words, fill in the number of morphemes and write the free and bound morphemes in the appropriate blanks. The first one is done for you.

| WORD | # OF MORPHEMES | FREE | BOUND |
|---|---|---|---|
| 1. eraser | 2 | erase | -er |
| 2. wicked | | | |
| 3. invalid (A) | | | |
| 4. invalid (N) | | | |
| 5. Jack's | | | |
| 6. optionality | | | |
| 7. refurnish | | | |
| 8. inabilities | | | |
| 9. denationalize | | | |
| 10. deride | | | |
| 11. activation | | | |

# IDENTIFYING LEXICAL CATEGORIES (Section 1.2, pp. 135–137)

In morphology, we are concerned with four lexical categories: nouns, verbs, adjectives, and prepositions. Nouns typically refer to concrete and abstract objects; verbs typically denote actions or states; adjectives typically refer to properties of nouns; and prepositions typically indicate relations in space or time.

## PRACTICE 4.3: Lexical categories

For each of the following words, fill in the number of morphemes, and identify the root, the lexical category of the root, and the lexical category of the entire word. Be careful: The root's lexical category and the word's lexical category may or may not be the same. The first one is done for you.

| WORD | # OF MORPHEMES | ROOT | ROOT CATEGORY | WORD CATEGORY |
|------|------|------|------|------|
| 1. kindnesses | 3 | kind | adjective | noun |
| 2. amazement | | | | |
| 3. reusable | | | | |
| 4. dishonest | | | | |
| 5. Baltimore | | | | |
| 6. lovelier | | | | |
| 7. historical | | | | |
| 8. uncontrolled | | | | |
| 9. impersonal | | | | |
| 10. trees | | | | |
| 11. faster | | | | |
| 12. rereads | | | | |
| 13. beautiful | | | | |
| 14. child | | | | |

# WORD TREES (Section 1.2, pp. 135–137)

A word tree is a representation of how a word was put together. To put together a word tree, you need to be able to identify the number of morphemes in a word, including roots, affixes and lexical categories.

Below are some examples of how to draw a word tree.

1. Words with a single affix.

    a.

```
A
|
kindness
```

```
    N
   / \
  A   Af
  |   |
kindness
```

     1. Identify the root and determine its lexical category.

     2. Attach the suffix and determine the lexical category of the resulting word. This may or may not be the same as the lexical category of the root.

    b.

```
A
|
unkind
```

```
   A
  / \
 Af  A
 |   |
unkind
```

     1. Identify the root and determine its lexical category.

     2. Attach the prefix and determine the lexical category of the resulting word. This is typically the same as the lexical category of the root.

2.  Words with multiple suffixes.

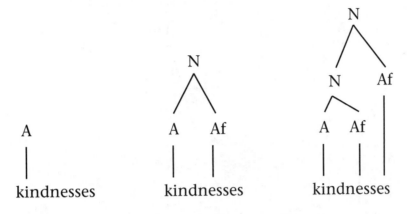

1.  Identify the root and determine its lexical category.

2.  Attach the first affix and determine the lexical category of the resulting word.

3.  Attach the next affix and determine the lexical category of the resulting word.

3.  Words with both a prefix and a suffix.

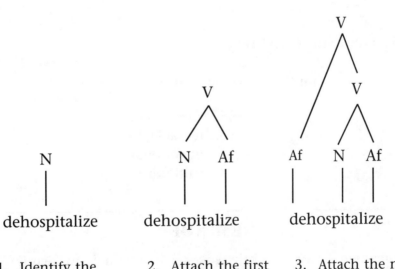

1.  Identify the root and determine its lexical category.

2.  Attach the first affix and determine the lexical category of the resulting word.

3.  Attach the next affix and determine the lexical category of the resulting word.

4. Words that are structurally ambiguous.

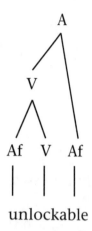

The prefix *un* is first attached to create the verb *unlock*. The suffix *able* is then attached to create the adjective *unlockable*.

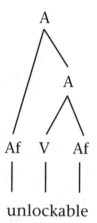

The suffix *able* is first attached to create the adjective *lockable*. The prefix *un* is then attached to create the adjective *unlockable*.

## PRACTICE 4.4: Drawing word trees

To practice, draw word trees for the following words:

1. trees
2. lovelier
3. dishonest
4. beautiful
5. amazement
6. reusable
7. impersonal
8. Baltimore

---

### REMINDER

To be able to draw word trees correctly, you need to be able to identify nouns, verbs, adjectives, and prepositions. If you are having difficulty with these, get some help.

---

# INFLECTION (Section 5, pp. 155–158)

Inflection is sometimes a process of affixation. As will be discussed further, inflection can also be a process of internal change as well as a process of suppletion. Affixation is a morphological process that adds affixes to words. Inflectional affixes are affixes that:

- function to provide grammatical information
- never change the lexical category of a word
- occur at the outer edges of a word (e.g., last)

English has eight inflectional affixes. They are found on nouns, verbs, and adjectives.

## NOUNS

1. PLURAL:     -s
dogs, cats, roses

2. POSSESSIVE:     -'s
Mary's book, Pat's book, the judge's book

## VERBS

1. THIRD-PERSON SINGULAR:     -s
She likes jazz. He walks slowly. He hisses loudly.

2. PAST TENSE:     -ed
She filled the gas tank. He wanted a dog.

3. PROGRESSIVE:     -ing
I am sighing. You are singing. He is walking.
We are talking. He was sighing. They were leaving.

4. PAST PARTICIPLE:     -en / -ed
I have spoken. He has filled the gas tank.

## ADJECTIVES

1. COMPARATIVE:     -er
greener, louder, faster, softer

2. SUPERLATIVE:     -est
greenest, loudest, fastest, softest

## PRACTICE 4.5: Recognizing lexical categories and inflection

For each of the following words, identify the lexical category of the root and the type of inflectional information found (e.g., past tense, superlative, plural). The first one is done for you.

| WORD | LEXICAL CATEGORY | INFLECTIONAL INFORMATION |
|---|---|---|
| 1. watched | verb | past tense |
| 2. runs | | |
| 3. sorriest | | |
| 4. lamps | | |
| 5. playing | | |
| 6. driven | | |
| 7. lovelier | | |
| 8. dishes | | |

# DERIVATION (Section 2, pp. 142–147)

Derivation is also a process of affixation. Again, affixation is a process that adds affixes to words. Derivational affixes are affixes that:

- build words having a different (but usually related) semantic content than the base
- usually change the lexical category of a word
- occur closer to the root than do inflectional affixes

English has many derivational affixes. Below are some examples of English derivational suffixes. English derivational suffixes have all the characteristics of derivation given above.

### SUFFIXES

| Affix | Change | Semantic Effect | Example |
|---|---|---|---|
| -able | V → Adj | able to be X'ed | affordable |
| -ant | V → N | one who X's | participant |
| -ation | V → N | the result of X'ing | organization |
| -er | V → N | one who X's | employer |
| -ing | V → N | the act of X'ing | the singing |
| | V → Adj | the process of X'ing | the crying baby |
| -ion | V → N | the result or act of X'ing | reflection |

| Affix | Change | Semantic Effect | Example |
|-------|--------|-----------------|---------|
| -ive | V → Adj | having the property of doing X | combative |
| -ment | V → N | the act or result of X'ing | postponement |
| -al | N → Adj | pertaining to X | original |
| -ial | N → Adj | pertaining to X | racial |
| -ian | N → Adj | pertaining to X | Brazilian |
| -ic | N → Adj | having the property of X | idiotic |
| -ful | N → Adj | having X | skillful |
| -ize | N → V | put in X | hospitalize |
|  | Adj → V | make X | criminalize |
| -less | N → Adj | without X | hopeless |
| -ous | N → Adj | the property of having or being X | humorous |
| -ate | Adj → V | make X | validate |
| -en | Adj → V | make X | fatten |
| -ity | Adj → N | the result of being X | morality |
| -y | N → Adj | being like X | gravelly |
| -ness | Adj → N | the state of being X | kindness |

English also has many derivational prefixes; however, these do not change lexical category. Despite this, English prefixes are still considered derivational. This is because of the semantic change that occurs when they are used during word formation.

## PREFIXES

| Affix | Change | Semantic Effect | Example |
|-------|--------|-----------------|---------|
| anti- | N → N | against X | anti-war |
| ex- | N → N | former X | ex-boyfriend |
| in- | Adj → Adj | not X | incomplete |
| un- | Adj → Adj | not X | unworthy |
|  | V → V | reverse X | unlock |
| de- | V → V | reverse X | desensitize |
| dis- | V → V | reverse X | disconnect |
| re- | V → V | X again | remarry |

## PRACTICE 4.6: Identifying affixes
(Section 1.1, pp. 133–135; Section 5.2, pp. 156–158)

For each of the following English words, state whether it is simple or complex. If it is complex, state whether the affix is inflectional or derivational. The first one is done for you.

| WORD | SIMPLE / COMPLEX | INFL / DERIV |
|---|---|---|
| 1. desks | | |
| 2. fly | complex | inflectional |
| 3. prettier | | |
| 4. stringy | | |
| 5. delight | | |
| 6. reuse | | |
| 7. triumphed (past) | | |
| 8. fastest | | |
| 9. mistreat | | |

# FORM VS. FUNCTION

Many affixes have the same form, but different functions. That is, affixes having the same form can be either inflectional or derivational, or they can be different inflectional affixes or derivational affixes. You need to be able to identify affixes according to their function rather than by their form. The following exercise should help.

## PRACTICE 4.7: Form vs. function of affixes

In each of the following groups of words, two words have the same type of affix, one word has a different affix, and one word has no affix at all. Underline the affix in each word. Then, next to each word, write S (same), D (different), or N (none), based on the items in the set. You may want to use a dictionary. The first one is done for you.

1.  oven<u>s</u>       ___S___        5.  greener      _____
    lens        ___N___            farmer       _____
    hen<u>s</u>       ___S___            colder       _____
    listen<u>s</u>    ___D___            water        _____

2.  greedy      _____        6.  friendly     _____
    ivory       _____            slowly       _____
    jealousy    _____            intelligently _____
    dirty       _____            early        _____

3.  leaven      _____        7.  intelligent  _____
    harden      _____            inhale       _____
    spoken      _____            incongruous  _____
    thicken     _____            inhuman      _____

4.  rider       _____        8.  candied      _____
    colder      _____            shopped      _____
    silver      _____            cleaned      _____
    actor       _____            candid       _____

# COMPOUNDING (Section 3, pp. 147–151)

Compounding is another morphological process. Compounding involves the combination of two or more words into a new word. There are three important properties of English compounds:

- **Stress patterns.** Even though compounds can be spelled as one word, two words, or with a hyphen separating the morphemes, a generalization can be made about the stress patterns found on them. Stress tends to be more prominent on the first member of the compound rather than the second. For example, *greénhouse* (a garden center) versus *green hoúse* (a house that is green).

- **Headedness.** The head of a compound is the morpheme that determines the category of the entire compound. Most English compounds are right-headed. That is, the category of the entire compound is the same as the category of the rightmost member of the compound. For example, the compound *blackboard* is a noun, since the rightmost member *board* is a noun.

- **Semantic patterns.** Compounds are used to express a wide range of meaning relationships. Many compounds are endocentric. In an endocentric compound, the entire compound denotes a subtype of the head. For example, a *teacup* is a type of *cup*, and a *lunchroom* is a type of *room*. Some compounds are exocentric. In an exocentric compound the meaning of the compound does not come from the head. For example, a *redneck* is not a type of *neck*, but a type of person.

## PRACTICE 4.8: Compounds

For each of the following compounds, identify the lexical categories making it up and give another example of that type of compound. Give a different example for each compound. The first one is done for you.

| COMPOUND | LEXICAL CATEGORIES | EXAMPLE |
|---|---|---|
| 1. bathroom | noun + noun | movie star |
| 2. scarecrow | | |
| 3. skin-deep | | |
| 4. bittersweet | | |
| 5. upstairs | | |

Now go back and draw a word tree for each compound.

# WORD TREES TO SHOW INFLECTION, DERIVATION, AND COMPOUNDING (Section 1.2, pp. 135–137; Section 2.1, pp. 143–146; Section 3, pp. 147–148; Section 5.2, pp. 156–158)

Remember that more than one process can be used to build a single word. A word like *black-boards*, for example, is a compound noun (*black + board*) with an inflectional suffix *-s* for the plural. If you are in doubt about the lexical category of an entire word, you can look at the affixes; sentence context can also help you determine the lexical category.

For example, the tree for the word *workable* as in the sentence *I like the workable solution* might be diagrammed as follows:

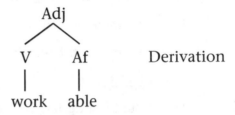

## PRACTICE 4.9: Drawing word trees

Draw one tree diagram for each of the following words, and identify whether inflection, derivation, and/or compounding was used to build the word.

| | WORD | CONTEXT SENTENCE |
|---|---|---|
| 1. | taken | The baby has <u>taken</u> his first steps. |
| 2. | spoonfeeding | Mother is <u>spoonfeeding</u> the baby. |
| 3. | softest | The <u>softest</u> pillow has the |
| 4. | silkiest | <u>silkiest</u> cover. |
| 5. | introductions | Mary performed the <u>introductions</u>. |
| 6. | steps | John <u>steps</u> up the ladder. |
| 7. | steps | I hate those steep <u>steps</u>. |
| 8. | stringier | My hair is <u>stringier</u> than hers. |
| 9. | skiers | The <u>skiers</u> were rich. |
| 10. | father | My <u>father</u> lives in France. |
| 11. | stone cold | Your french fries are <u>stone cold</u>. |
| 12. | making | Jill is <u>making</u> candy. |
| 13. | boxing | We watched the <u>boxing</u> on television. |

| WORD | CONTEXT SENTENCE |
|---|---|
| 14. criticize | You <u>criticize</u> too much. |
| 15. creamy | <u>Creamy</u> chocolate is delicious. |
| 16. keepers | The <u>keepers</u> locked up for the night. |
| 17. blessing | Give me your <u>blessing</u>. |
| 18. blessing | She is <u>blessing</u> the bread. |
| 19. schoolteacher | My mother was a <u>schoolteacher</u>. |
| 20. clumsiness | I detest <u>clumsiness</u>. |
| 21. windmills | Holland has lots of <u>windmills</u>. |
| 22. hammered | John <u>hammered</u> on the door. |
| 23. thickeners | There are many different types of <u>thickeners</u>. |
| 24. unlocked | We <u>unlocked</u> the door. |
| 25. declaw | You should not <u>declaw</u> your cat. |
| 26. retry | She should <u>retry</u> the recipe. |
| 27. inside | The cat is <u>inside</u> the box. |
| 28. impure | <u>Impure</u> water is dangerous. |
| 29. sleepwalking | George is often found <u>sleepwalking</u>. |
| 30. defrosting | The steaks are <u>defrosting</u>. |

---

## REMINDER

Remember that *all* English prefixes are derivational even though they do not cause a lexical category change.

---

# OTHER MORPHOLOGICAL PROCESSES (Section 1.3, pp. 137–142)

Other common morphological processes found in the world's languages include:

| PROCESS | DEFINITION |
|---|---|
| Cliticization | Clitics are short unstressed words that must be pronounced with another word. In English, these are reduced forms that cannot be pronounced as a stand-alone word, since they no longer constitute a syllable. Clitics differ from affixes in that clitics are members of a lexical category (e.g., noun [or pronoun], verb).<br><br>e.g., *'re* from *are* as in *they're* |
| Internal Change | This process provides grammatical information by changing a portion of the morpheme. That is, the tense or number of a word is marked by changing a sound within the morpheme.<br><br>e.g., *run → ran* |
| Reduplication | A process that copies all (full) or a portion (partial) of the base to mark a semantic or grammatical contrast.<br><br>This process has only limited use in English.<br><br>e.g., Turkish: [iji] 'well' → [iji] [iji] 'very well'<br>Tagalog: [lakad] 'walk' → [lalakad] 'will walk' |
| Stress Placement | A change in the stress placement that causes a change in the lexical category of a word.<br><br>e.g., *recórd* (verb) → *récord* (noun) |
| Suppletion | This process provides grammatical information by changing the entire morpheme. That is, the tense, number, etc., of a word is marked by replacing one morpheme with an entirely different morpheme.<br><br>e.g., *go → went* |
| Tone Placement | This process is similar to stress placement in that a difference in tone can be used to create different words, or to mark a change in tense or number. This process is found in tone languages.<br><br>e.g., Mono-Bili: Past (high tone)    Future (low tone)<br>*dá* 'spanked'    *dà* 'will spank'<br>*wó* 'killed'    *wò* 'will kill' |

# OTHER WORD-FORMATION PROCESSES (Section 5, pp. 151–155)

In addition to derivation and compounding, other common word-building processes include:

| PROCESS | DEFINITION |
|---|---|
| Conversion | A process that assigns an existing word to a different lexical category.     e.g., *butter* (N) → *(to) butter* (V) |
| Clipping | A process that shortens a word by removing one or more syllables. e.g., *condominium* → *condo* |
| Blending | A process that creates a new word by combining portions of two existing words.     e.g., *spiced + ham* → *spam* |
| Backformation | A process that creates a word by removing a supposed affix from an existing word.     e.g., *enthusiasm* → *enthuse* |
| Acronym | A new word created by using the initial letters of the words in a phrase or title.     e.g., *scuba, Unicef* |
| Onomatopoeia | Words that have been created to sound like the thing they name. e.g., *buzz, hiss, sizzle* |
| Coinage | A process that creates a totally new word.     e.g., *Teflon* |

## PRACTICE 4.10: Word-formation processes

Identify the process responsible for the formation of each of the following English words. Choose from any of the morphological and word-formation processes in the preceding two tables as well as inflection, derivation, and compounding. The first one is done for you.

1. infomercial                 _____blending_____

2. (to) ship                 _____

3. mice                 _____

4. support hose                 _____

5. chirp                 _____

6. drove                 _____

7.  healthy          _____

8.  demo             _____

9.  better           _____

10. teeth            _____

11. he's             _____

12. headline         _____

13. repórt           _____

14. beep             _____

15. ATM              _____

There are many examples of different word-formation processes in the following passage. Find all the examples of acronym, backformation, blending, clipping, coinage, and compounding.

John didn't enthuse about UCLA, as he probably expected his profs to spoonfeed him. He preferred to avoid the smog by taking sandwiches to the beach, where he would laze around and go scuba diving in his new dacron dry suit. One day he was suffering from a headache and dizziness, which he thought might be caused by sunstroke or the flu, so he went to the doctor. The doc sent him to the lab for a urinalysis and a blood test and suggested that he should see an ENT specialist as well. He is now OK, having returned from LA, and he is learning about ohms, watts, and volts at MIT.

# INTRODUCTION TO MORPHOLOGY PROBLEMS

The goal in tackling morphology problems is to isolate and identify all the morphemes in the data given. To do this, you must identify recurring strings of sounds and match them with recurring meanings. It sounds harder than it really is. Here are a few easy ones to try.

## PRACTICE 4.11: Easy morphology problems

All data are given in phonetic transcription.

1. **Mende** (Sierra Leone)

   | | | | | |
   |---|---|---|---|---|
   | 1. | [pɛlɛ] | 'house' | [pɛlɛi] | 'the house' |
   | 2. | [mɔm] | 'glass' | [mɔmi] | 'the glass' |
   | 3. | [dɔmi] | 'story' | [dɔmii] | 'the story' |
   | 4. | [kali] | 'hoe' | [kalii] | 'the hoe' |
   | 5. | [hele] | 'elephant' | [helei] | 'the elephant' |
   | 6. | [kaamɔ] | 'teacher' | [kaamɔi] | 'the teacher' |
   | 7. | [navo] | 'boy' | [navoi] | 'the boy' |
   | 8. | [numu] | 'person' | [numui] | 'the person' |

   a. What is the morpheme meaning 'the'? _____

   b. If [sale] means 'proverb', what is the form for 'the proverb'? _____

   c. If [kpindii] means 'the night', what does [kpindi] mean? _____

2. **Ganda** (Uganda)

   | | | | | |
   |---|---|---|---|---|
   | 1. | [omukazi] | 'woman' | [abakazi] | 'women' |
   | 2. | [omusawo] | 'doctor' | [abasawo] | 'doctors' |
   | 3. | [omusika] | 'heir' | [abasika] | 'heirs' |
   | 4. | [omuwala] | 'girl' | [abawala] | 'girls' |
   | 5. | [omulenzi] | 'boy' | [abalenzi] | 'boys' |

   a. What is the morpheme meaning SINGULAR? _____

   b. What is the morpheme meaning PLURAL? _____

   c. If [abalanga] means 'twins', what is the form for 'twin'? _____

3. **Kanuri**

| | | | | |
|---|---|---|---|---|
| 1. | [gana] | 'small' | [nəmgana] | 'smallness' |
| 2. | [kura] | 'big' | [nəmkura] | 'bigness' |
| 3. | [kurugu] | 'long' | [nəmkurugu] | 'length' |
| 4. | [karite] | 'excellent' | [nəmkarite] | 'excellence' |
| 5. | [dibi] | 'bad' | [nəmdibi] | 'badness' |

a. What type of affix is shown (i.e., prefix, suffix, infix)? _____

b. What is the affix? _____

c. If [kəji] means 'sweet', what is the form for 'sweetness'? _____

d. If [nəmgəla] means 'goodness', what is the form for 'good'? _____

e. What word-formation process is evident in the data? _____

f. Draw a word tree for [nəmkurugu] 'length'.

## PRACTICE 4.12: More morphology problems

The following pages contain somewhat more difficult problems based on data sets from different languages. These data sets are intended to give you practice in doing morphological analysis. Each contains sufficient data to make valid conclusions; however, the data may have been regularized somewhat. Data are in phonetic transcription unless otherwise noted.

1. **Toba Batak**
   Toba Batak is a Malayo-Polynesian language of Sumatra. Although tones are marked, you may disregard them for this exercise.

| | | | | |
|---|---|---|---|---|
| 1. | [deŋgán] | 'good' | [duméŋgan] | 'better' |
| 2. | [tíbbo] | 'tall' | [tumíbbo] | 'taller' |
| 3. | [rɔá] | 'ugly' | [rumɔa] | 'uglier' |
| 4. | [gokan] | 'full' | [gumokán] | 'fuller' |
| 5. | [rahis] | 'steep' | [rumáhis] | 'steeper' |
| 6. | [holom] | 'dark' | [humolom] | 'darker' |

a. What morpheme indicates the comparative? _____

b. What kind of affix is this morpheme? _____

c. If [datu] means 'wise', what is the form for 'wiser'? _____

d. If [sɔmal] means 'usual', what is the form for 'more usual'? _____

e. If [ʤumɛppɛk] means 'shorter', what is the form for 'short'? _____

f. If [lumógo] means 'drier', what is the form for 'dry'? _____

2. **Turkish**

[y] represents a high front rounded vowel.

[œ] represents a mid front rounded vowel.

| | | | | | |
|---|---|---|---|---|---|
| 1. | [ʃehir] | 'city' | 10. | [zilim] | 'my bell' |
| 2. | [ʃehirden] | 'from the city' | 11. | [ziller] | 'bells' |
| 3. | [el] | 'hand' | 12. | [eve] | 'to the house' |
| 4. | [elim] | 'my hand' | 13. | [evde] | 'in the house' |
| 5. | [elimde] | 'in my hand' | 14. | [evden] | 'from the house' |
| 6. | [kœpry] | 'bridge' | 15. | [kœpryden] | 'from the bridge' |
| 7. | [kœpryler] | 'bridges' | 16. | [ellerinize] | 'to your hands' |
| 8. | [kœprylere] | 'to the bridges' | 17. | [sesleriniz] | 'your voices' |
| 9. | [kœpryde] | 'on the bridge' | 18. | [otobysler] | 'buses' |

a. What morphemes mean:

1. city _____

2. hand _____

3. bridge _____

4. bell _____

5. house _____

6. voice _____

7. bus _____

8. from _____

9. to _____

10. on, in _____

11. my _____

12. your _____

13. PLURAL _____

b. What is the order of morphemes?

Fill in the boxes with: PLURAL, POSSESSIVE, POSTPOSITION, ROOT

| | | | |
|---|---|---|---|
| | | | |

c. What do the following mean in English?

1. [ʃehirde] _____

2. [elleriniz] _____

d. How would you say 'to the buses' in Turkish? _____

3. **Classical Nahuatl**
Nahuatl is an Aztecan language of Mexico.

| | | | | | |
|---|---|---|---|---|---|
| 1. | [tikʷiːka] | 'you (SG) sing' | 8. | [kikʷa] | 'he eats it' |
| 2. | [kʷiːka] | 's/he sings' | 9. | [kikʷaʔ] | 'they eat it' |
| 3. | [tikʷiːkaʔ] | 'we sing' | 10. | [aːltia] | 'he bathes' |
| 4. | [ankʷiːkaʔ] | 'you (PL) sing' | 11. | [aːltiaʔ] | 'they bathe' |
| 5. | [kʷiːkaʔ] | 'they sing' | 12. | [kikʷaːni] | 'he customarily eats it' |
| 6. | [kʷa] | 'he eats' | 13. | [aːltiaːni] | 'he customarily  bathes' |
| 7. | [kʷaʔ] | 'they eat' | 14. | [tiaːltiaːni] | 'you (SG) customarily bathe' |

a. What are the morphemes for:

   1. sing                       _____

   2. eat                        _____

   3. bathe                    _____

   4. you (SG) (subject)      _____

   5. s/he (subject)          _____

   6. it (object)             _____

   7. we (subject)           _____

   8. you (PL) (subject)     _____

   9. they (subject)         _____

b. What is the suffix that marks a plural subject in the present? _____

c. How is the customary present marked? _____

---

**REMINDERS**

1.  An affix is an infix only when it is inserted into a root.
2.  Don't forget to use morphological boundary markers (i.e., hyphens) for all bound affixes (prefixes, suffixes, and affixes). Root words do not need morphological boundaries.

# MORPHOPHONEMICS (Section 7, pp. 164–169)

Morphemes do not always have the same form. Allomorphs are the different forms of a morpheme. Consider the following English example.

- **The Allomorphs:** The English plural morpheme *-s* has three different phonetic forms:

    [-s] in words like *cats*
    [-z] in words like *dogs*
    [-əz] in words like *dishes*

- **The Conditioning Environment:** Which phonetic form is realized depends on the phonological characteristics of the final segment in the preceding word:

    [-s] occurs after a base ending in a voiceless consonant that is not strident
    [-z] occurs after a base ending in a voiced segment that is not strident
    [-əz] occurs after a base ending in a strident consonant

The specific environment in which the different allomorphs occur is often referred to as the distribution of the allomorphs. This interaction between morphology and phonology is called **morphophonemics**.

- **The Underlying Representation:** One allomorph is selected as the underlying representation of the morpheme. This is typically the allomorph that has the widest distribution.

    [-z] is selected as the underlying representation, since it occurs after the most sounds (voiced consonants and vowels, which are also voiced)

- **The Derivation:** Rules are required to derive the correct phonetic form from the underlying representation.

    | | |
    |---|---|
    | Coda epenthesis: | Insert a schwa whenever [-z] occurs after a base that ends in a strident sound. |
    | Devoicing: | Devoice [-z] after a voiceless consonant in the same coda. |

These rules are often a reflection of the phonological processes at work in the pronunciation of the morphemes. And just like in phonology, rules must sometimes be ordered so that the correct phonetic form is derived. Coda epenthesis must occur before devoicing. If the devoicing rule occurs first, then [-z] becomes voiceless and epenthesis fails to apply.

## PRACTICE 4.13: Morphophonemics

Spot the allomorphs in the following exercises, and answer the questions that follow.

1. **English**

    | | | | | |
    |---|---|---|---|---|
    | 1. | [ɪnɛdɪbəl] | 'inedible' | 5. [ɪnsəpɔrtəbəl] | 'insupportable' |
    | 2. | [ɪmpɑsɪbəl] | 'impossible' | 6. [ɪnəbɪləti] | 'inability' |
    | 3. | [ɪŋkejpəbəl] | 'incapable' | 7. [ɪmɔrəl] | 'immoral' |
    | 4. | [ɪntɑlərənt] | 'intolerant' | 8. [ɪŋkəmplit] | 'incomplete' |

a. What are the three different allomorphs of the morpheme meaning 'not'?

_____

State the environment (in words) in which the allomorphs occur.

1. _____

2. _____

3. _____

b. Which allomorph would you choose as the underlying representation of the morpheme?

_____

c. Give the underlying representation of the words *inedible*, *impossible*, and *incapable*.

_____

d. What phonological process is at work in the data?

_____

e. What are the rules you would need to derive the phonetic forms? Do these rules need to be ordered?

_____

2. **Turkish**
Vowel harmony is a process that results in all vowels of a word sharing a certain feature or features. Morphophonemic rules of vowel harmony are found in many languages. Look at the data from Turkish and answer the following questions.
[y] represents a high front rounded vowel.
[œ] represents a mid front rounded vowel.

| | | | | | | |
|---|---|---|---|---|---|---|
| 1. | [gœz] | 'eye' | | [gœzler] | 'eyes' |
| 2. | [mum] | 'candle' | | [mumlɑr] | 'candles' |
| 3. | [top] | 'gun' | | [toplɑr] | 'guns' |
| 4. | [at] | 'horse' | | [atlɑr] | 'horses' |
| 5. | [ip] | 'thread' | | [ipler] | 'threads' |
| 6. | [gyl] | 'rose' | | [gyller] | 'roses' |
| 7. | [mektup] | 'letter' | | [mektuplɑr] | 'letters' |
| 8. | [anne] | 'mother' | | [anneler] | 'mothers' |
| 9. | [limɑn] | 'harbor' | | [limɑnlɑr] | 'harbors' |
| 10. | [ʃule] | 'flame' | | [ʃuleler] | 'flames' |

a. What are the allomorphs of the plural morpheme? _____ _____

b. What phonological feature distinguishes the vowels of the allomorphs?

_____

c. What feature of the last vowel in the root determines the choice of the plural

allomorph? _____

3. **Dutch**

In Dutch, there are "strong verbs" and "weak verbs" depending on the form of the past tense and past participle (the past participle is the verb form used with *have* in English, e.g., *has <u>done</u>*). Examine the data from Dutch, which is in Dutch orthography, and answer the following questions.

**WEAK VERBS**

| <u>Root</u> | <u>Infinitive</u> | <u>Past Participle</u> | |
|---|---|---|---|
| werk | werken | gewerkt | 'work' |
| luister | luisteren | geluisterd | 'listen' |
| poets | poetsen | gepoetst | 'brush' |
| winkel | winkelen | gewinkeld | 'go shopping' |
| regen | regenen | geregend | 'rain' |
| fietst | fietsten | gefietst | 'bike' (i.e., go by bicycle) |
| zag | zagen | gezagd | 'saw, harp on something' |

**STRONG VERBS**

| <u>Infinitive</u> | <u>Past Participle</u> | |
|---|---|---|
| bijten | gebeten | 'bite' |
| laten | gelaten | 'let, leave off' |
| sterven | gestorven | 'die from' |
| nemen | genomen | 'take' |

a. How is the infinitive formed for weak verbs in Dutch? _____

b. How is the past participle formed for weak verbs in Dutch? _____

What are the two forms of the past participle of the weak verb?

_____  _____

Under what conditions is each form used?

_____  _____

c. Interestingly, the two forms of the past participle of the weak verb in Dutch are pronounced the same. What do you think is the pronunciation, and what phonological process has occurred? _____

d. Strong verbs undergo internal change, which need not concern us here. What affix is

added to form the past participle of strong verbs in Dutch? _____

e. *Iemand <u>heeft mijn auto gestolen</u>* means 'Someone <u>has stolen my car</u>.' Is *gestolen* a weak

verb or a strong verb? How do you know? _____

## REVIEW EXERCISES

The following exercises will provide review in solving morphology problems.

1. **Ancient Egyptian**
   Ancient Egyptian was written in hieroglyphics (see Chapter 15 in the main text). We do not know how the vowels were pronounced, so it is transliterated without vowels. The following data have been transcribed with IPA symbols instead of the traditional orthography for ancient Egyptian.

   [tʲ]  represents a palatalized [t].

   | | | | | | |
   |---|---|---|---|---|---|
   | 1. | sn | 'brother' | snwj | '2 brothers' | snw | 'brothers' |
   | 2. | snt | 'sister' | sntj | '2 sisters' | snwt | 'sisters' |
   | 3. | ntʲr | 'god' | ntʲrwj | '2 gods' | ntʲrw | 'gods' |
   | 4. | ntʲrt | 'goddess' | ntʲrtj | '2 goddesses' | ntʲrwt | 'goddesses' |

   a.  What morphemes mean:

   1. sibling        _____

   2. deity          _____

   3. FEMININE       _____

   4. MASCULINE      _____

   5. DUAL           _____

   6. PLURAL         _____

   b.  What is the order of morphemes?
       Fill in the boxes with terms from this list: DUAL, FEMININE, PLURAL, ROOT

   1. M SG   [          ]

   2. F SG   [          ][          ]

   3. M PL   [          ][          ]

   4. F PL   [          ][          ][          ]

   5. M DU   [          ][          ][          ]

   6. F DU   [          ][          ][          ]

2. **Luganda**

Luganda is a Bantu language of eastern Africa.

| | | | |
|---|---|---|---|
| 1. [muntu] | 'person' | 11. [musege] | 'wolf' |
| 2. [kati] | 'stick' | 12. [bawala] | 'girls' |
| 3. [kitabo] | 'book' | 13. [kugulu] | 'leg' |
| 4. [bitabo] | 'books' | 14. [katiko] | 'mushroom' |
| 5. [magulu] | 'legs' | 15. [matu] | 'ears' |
| 6. [miti] | 'trees' | 16. [buti] | 'sticks' |
| 7. [muti] | 'tree' | 17. [bintu] | 'things' |
| 8. [kutu] | 'ear' | 18. [muwala] | 'girl' |
| 9. [butiko] | 'mushrooms' | 19. [misege] | 'wolves' |
| 10. [kintu] | 'thing' | 20. [bantu] | 'people' |

Five noun classes are represented here according to the forms for singular and plural. Fill in the following chart. In the boxes labeled "CLASS," give an arbitrary number to the class. For each class, in the box labeled "SG," write the morpheme for the singular. In the box labeled "PL," write the morpheme for the plural. In the box labeled "STEMS," write the stems (the morphemes without the singular or plural), and in the corresponding space in the box labeled "GLOSS," write the meaning of the stem between single quotes. Some of the data have been filled in for you.

| CLASS | SG | PL | STEMS | GLOSS |
|---|---|---|---|---|
| 1 | mu- | ba- | | |
| | | | | |
| | | | | |
| | | | | |
| | | | | |

3. **Fore**

| | | | | |
|---|---|---|---|---|
| 1. [natuwi] | 'I ate yesterday.' | | 8. [natuni] | 'We ate yesterday.' |
| 2. [nagasuwi] | 'I ate today.' | | 9. [nagasuni] | 'We ate today.' |
| 3. [nakuwi] | 'I will eat.' | | 10. [nagasusi] | 'We (DUAL) ate today.' |
| 4. [nata:ni] | 'You ate yesterday.' | | 11. [nakuni] | 'We will eat.' |
| 5. [nata:naw] | 'You ate yesterday?' | | 12. [nakusi] | 'We (DUAL) will eat.' |
| 6. [nakiyi] | 'He will eat.' | | 13. [nata:wi] | 'They ate yesterday.' |
| 7. [nakiyaw] | 'He will eat?' | | 14. [nata:si] | 'They (DUAL) ate yesterday.' |

- Don't forget that what are inflectional affixes in many languages can be translated into separate words in English.

- 'Yesterday,' 'today,' and 'tomorrow' are translations of the English past, present, and future tenses (respectively).

a. Identify the Fore morphemes that correspond to the following English words:

| | | | |
|---|---|---|---|
| 1. I | _____ | 7. eat | _____ |
| 2. he | _____ | 8. yesterday | _____ |
| 3. we | _____ | 9. today | _____ |
| 4. they | _____ | 10. will | _____ |
| 5. we (DUAL) | _____ | 11. question | _____ |
| 6. they (DUAL) | _____ | 12. statement | _____ |

b. Describe the order of the morphemes in terms of personal pronouns, question/statement markers, verbs, and adverbs.

c. Give the Fore words for the following:

1. He ate yesterday?   _____

2. They (DUAL) will eat?   _____

3. They ate today.   _____

**RECAP**

Make sure you know how to do the following. (See also the Key Terms on pp. 169–170 of the main text.)

- define morphological terms
- divide a word into its morphemes
- assign lexical categories
- build word trees
- identify inflection and derivation
- construct compound words
- recognize endocentric and exocentric compounds
- recognize morphological and word-formation processes
- do morphological analysis
- identify word-formation processes in unfamiliar languages
- find and derive allomorphs

## QUESTIONS? PROBLEMS?

*five*

# SYNTAX: THE ANALYSIS OF SENTENCE STRUCTURE

Syntax is the study of the system of rules and categories that underlies sentence formation. Following are some of the important topics and concepts covered in this chapter. Make sure you are familiar with them.

Syntactic categories
Phrases
Phrase structure rules
Phrase structure tests
Phrase structure trees
Subcategorization
Simple sentences
Sentences with complement clauses
Model of the grammar
Transformations
Universal Grammar and variation

## SYNTACTIC CATEGORIES (Section 1.1, pp. 185–187)

There are two types of syntactic categories: lexical and nonlexical. Nonlexical categories are sometimes called functional categories. Some of the major characteristics of each include:

**Lexical:**
- words that have semantic content
- words that can be inflected
- an open class to which new members can be added
- includes nouns, verbs, adjectives, adverbs, and prepositions
- often called the major classes

**Nonlexical:**
- words that have a grammatical function
- words that do not have morphology
- words that resist change
- a closed class to which new members are not added
- includes determiners, auxiliary verbs, degree words, qualifiers, pronouns, conjunctions, complementizers, and particles
- often called the minor classes

Make sure you understand the difference between the two types of lexical categories.

## PRACTICE 5.1: Syntactic categories

Each of the following sentences contains some underlined words. Identify the category of each underlined word. Note that the underlined word can be either lexical or nonlexical.

Words can often be assigned to more than one category, so pay close attention to how the word is being used in the sentence.

1. Pamela's heart <u>beat</u> fast <u>and</u> her hands trembled a lot as <u>she</u> listened <u>to</u> the intermittent knocking on <u>the</u> front <u>door</u> of her shanty, <u>located</u> near the railroad tracks beside a <u>hobo jungle</u>, and she thought, "That's a <u>bum</u> rap if I ever <u>heard</u> one."

2. "The <u>leg</u>, he is fractured," he <u>said</u> <u>in</u> broken English.

3. The Great Barrier Reef is 900 miles long, <u>and</u> Wilmer Chanti, <u>the</u> <u>great</u> <u>explorer</u>, <u>says</u> <u>it</u> <u>could</u> <u>be</u> circumnavigated <u>in</u> forty days.

4. When <u>I</u> <u>turned</u> the <u>key</u> to open my <u>lab</u> <u>door</u>, I <u>thought</u> it <u>would</u> be my usual <u>dull</u> <u>day</u>, until I <u>noticed</u> <u>that</u> <u>my</u> little cucaracha <u>had</u> <u>flopped</u> over on his back, frantically <u>waving</u> his little legs, and <u>I</u> <u>realized</u> that someone had bugged my bug.

5. It <u>was</u> a dark and stormy night, its <u>green</u> <u>clarity</u> <u>diluted</u> by my roommate who, as usual, <u>was</u> <u>making</u> <u>cutting</u> <u>remarks</u> as <u>she</u> <u>drank</u> my <u>scotch</u>.

6. "I <u>hate</u> <u>pineapples</u>," said Tom <u>dolefully</u>.

7. Here's how to make <u>a</u> <u>fortune</u>. Buy fifty <u>male</u> <u>deer</u>. Then <u>you</u> <u>will</u> <u>have</u> fifty <u>bucks</u>.

## PHRASES (Section 1.2, pp. 187–191)

Phrases consist of one or more words. There are three important properties of phrases.

- **Heads.** A phrase must have a head. The head of a phrase is the obligatory word after which the phrase is named and around which the phrase is built. Only lexical categories can be the head of a phrase. This allows for four possible types of phrases, as listed below.

  1. NP (noun phrase)
  2. AP (adjective phrase)
  3. VP (verb phrase)
  4. PP (prepositional phrase)

  The head of a noun phrase is, of course, a noun, the head of an adjective phrase, an adjective, and so on.

  There is actually a fifth type of phrase—the adverb phrase—which will not be examined in this chapter.

- **Specifiers.** A phrase can optionally contain a specifier. Specifiers help to make the meaning of the head more precise. In English, specifiers occur before the head, thus marking the beginning of a phrase. There are three types of specifiers in English:

    1. Det (determiners), which specify a noun
       e.g., *the, a, these, that*

    2. Qual (qualifiers), which specify a verb
       e.g., *always, often, never*

    3. Deg (degree words), which specify an adjective or a preposition
       e.g., *very, quite, really*

- **Complements.** A phrase can also optionally contain a complement. Complements provide more information about entities that are implied by the head of the phrase. In English, complements come after the head, thus marking the end of a phrase. Complements are typically other phrases.

Following are some examples of the four different types of phrases.

### 1. Noun Phrase (NP)

|   |   |   |
|---|---|---|
| a. | *presidents* | —contains only the head noun (*presidents*) |
| b. | *the presidents* | —contains a specifier (*the*) and the head noun (*presidents*) |
| c. | *presidents of the USA* | —contains the head noun (*presidents*) and a complement prepositional phrase (*of the USA*) |
| d. | *the presidents of the USA* | —contains a specifier (*the*), the head noun (*presidents*), and a complement prepositional phrase (*of the USA*) |

The complement prepositional phrase *of the USA* consists of a head preposition (*of*) and a complement noun phrase (*the USA*). The noun phrase *the USA* then consists of a specifier (*the*) and a head noun (*USA*).

### 2. Adjective Phrase (AP)

|   |   |   |
|---|---|---|
| a. | *happy* | —contains only the head adjective (*happy*) |
| b. | *very happy* | —contains a specifier (*very*) and the head adjective (*happy*) |
| c. | *happy with the results* | —contains the head adjective (*happy*) and a complement prepositional phrase (*with the results*) |
| d. | *very happy with the results* | —contains a specifier (*very*), the head adjective (*happy*), and a complement prepositional phrase (*with the results*) |

The complement prepositional phrase *with the results* consists of a head preposition (*with*) and a complement noun phrase (*the results*). The noun phrase *the results* then consists of a specifier (*the*) and a head noun (*results*).

---

### REMINDER

Phrases have hierarchical structure.

---

### 3. Verb Phrase (VP)

   a.  *sings*       —contains only the head verb (*sing*)

   b.  *often sings*    —contains a specifier (*often*) and the head verb (*sings*)

   c.  *sings a song*   —contains the head verb (*sing*) and a complement noun
                          phrase (*a song*)

   d.  *often sings*   —contains a specifier (*often*), the head verb (*sings*), and a
       *a song*        complement noun phrase (*a song*)

The complement noun phrase *a song* consists of a specifier (*a*) and a head noun (*song*).

### 4. Prepositional Phrase (PP)

   a.  *in the car*     —contains the head preposition (*in*) and a complement
                          noun phrase (*the car*)

   b.  *almost in*    —contains a specifier (*almost*), the head preposition (*in*),
       *the car*       and a complement noun phrase (*the car*)

The complement noun phrase *the car* contains a specifier (*the*) and a head noun (*car*).

Give an example of:

1. a noun phrase containing a specifier, a head noun, and a complement.
2. an adjective phrase containing a specifier and a head adjective.
3. a verb phrase containing a head verb and a complement.
4. a prepositional phrase containing a head preposition and a complement.

---

### REMINDER

Prepositional phrases are different from the other three types of phrases in that prepositional phrases must almost always contain a complement, and that complement is usually a noun phrase.

---

# PRACTICE 5.2: Heads, specifiers, and complements

For each of the following phrases, determine the head of the phrase, any specifiers, and any complements. Remember that every phrase must have a head. The first one is done for you.

|  | HEAD | SPECIFIER | COMPLEMENT |
|---|---|---|---|
| 1. the rat | rat | the | none |
| 2. men | | | |
| 3. in the barn | | | |
| 4. really mean | | | |
| 5. worked | | | |
| 6. worked at the station | | | |
| 7. extremely boring | | | |
| 8. that destruction of the city | | | |
| 9. never walks to the park | | | |
| 10. very small | | | |
| 11. in the room | | | |
| 12. awfully cute | | | |
| 13. seldom smiles | | | |
| 14. rather fond of apples | | | |
| 15. swept the floor | | | |
| 16. the poem about love | | | |
| 17. pancakes | | | |

Go back and determine the type of each phrase. Remember, the lexical category of the head determines the type of phrase.

# PHRASE STRUCTURE RULES (Section 1.2, pp. 187–191)

Phrase structure rules (PSR) describe the internal composition of a phrase. Phrase structure rules specify both the elements within a phrase and the order of those elements.

- **The general rule.** Remember that phrases consist of a head plus optional specifiers and/or complements. In English, specifiers come before the head, and complements come after the head. We can therefore construct one very general rule by which any English phrase can be generated:

$$XP \rightarrow \text{(specifier)} \quad X \quad \text{(complement)*}$$
$$\text{(where X can be any head)}$$

The left portion of the rule states the type of phrase that is being built. The right portion of the rule states both the elements and the order of the elements within the phrase. The parentheses ( ) indicate the optional elements. The asterisk * indicates that a phrase may have more than one complement.

- **More specific rules.** While the above rule is very general, more specific rules depicting the type of specifiers, modifiers and complements and heads within a particular phrase can also be written. For example, the rule for a noun phrase might look like this:

$$NP \rightarrow \text{(Det) N (PP)}$$

This rule states that within a noun phrase, determiners occupy the specifier position, and prepositional phrases occupy the complement position. It also states that within a noun phrase, both the specifier and the complement are optional.

## PRACTICE 5.3: Examples of PS rules

Give an example of a phrase that corresponds to each of the following rules.

1. AP → Deg A _____

2. VP → Qual V NP _____

3. VP → V NP _____

4. NP → N PP _____

5. NP → Det N _____

6. VP → V NP PP _____

7. AP → A PP _____

8. VP → Qual V PP _____

# PHRASE STRUCTURE TESTS (Section 1.4, pp. 193–194)

There are a number of tests that can be done to determine whether a group of words is or is not a syntactic unit (a constituent). Three frequently used tests are the substitution test, the movement test, and the coordination test.

## Substitution Test

The substitution test states that a group of words is a phrase if it can be substituted with a single word and still be grammatical. The word used as a substitute tells you the type of phrase you have.

NP:    A noun phrase can be substituted with a pronoun
> e.g., *The boys* played in the mud. *They* played in the mud.
> (*they = the boys*)

VP:    A verb phrase can be substituted with *do so*
> e.g., The girls will *play in the mud*, if the boys *do so*.
> (*do so = play in the mud*)

PP:    A prepositional phrase can sometimes be substituted with *there* or *them*
> e.g., The boys played *in the mud*. The boys played *there*.
> (*there = in the mud*)

## Movement Test

The movement test states that a group of words is a phrase if it can be moved to another position in the sentence and still be grammatical.

> e.g., The children bought candy *at the store*. ⟶
> *At the store*, the children bought candy.

## Coordination Test

According to this test, a group of words is a phrase if it can be joined to another group of words using a conjunction (*and, but, or*) and still be grammatical.

> e.g., The children *bought candy* and *left the store*.
> (two verb phrases joined with the conjunction *and*)

## PRACTICE 5.4: Phrase structure tests

1. Apply the substitution test to determine which of the bracketed sequences in the following sentences are phrases.

   1. [Juanita and Juan] arrived [in San Juan] [on Epiphany].
   2. The cabbage [rolls were] salty.
   3. They moved [the desk with the wooden top].
   4. Little Andrew swallowed [all the pills].
   5. Brendan is [writing a ballad about American soldiers in the Gulf].

2. Apply the movement test to determine which of the bracketed sequences in the following sentences are phrases.

   1. The [army was surrounded] by the enemy.
   2. Leona likes [Viennese waltzes and Argentinean tangos].
   3. Jean ate his lunch [in the revolving restaurant].
   4. Eat, drink, and [be merry for] today will become yesterday.
   5. The polar bears [were swimming across] the lake.

3. Use a conjunction (*and, but, or*) and join each of the following phrases with a phrase of the same type. Use the substitution test to determine the type of phrase.

   1. the new desk
   2. assembled the new desk
   3. new
   4. in a hole
   5. rather huge
   6. worked on a movie
   7. beside the fence
   8. really lovely
   9. talked to the girls
   10. a dentist

# PHRASE STRUCTURE TREES (Section 1.2, pp. 187–191)

Now that we know what the different types of phrases are and how to identify them, we are ready to start putting together phrase structure diagrams. Below is an example of a fully diagrammed noun phrase containing a head, a specifier, and a complement.

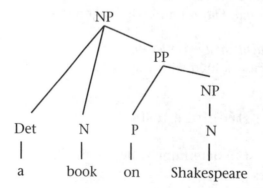

## PRACTICE 5.5: Drawing phrase structure trees

Draw tree diagrams for each of the following phrases. Remember, specifiers come before the head, and complements, after the head.

1. the rat
2. men
3. in the barn
4. really mean
5. ran
6. ran into the shed
7. extremely boring
8. hate those pancakes
9. the house on the corner
10. very small
11. in the room
12. awfully cute
13. seldom smiles
14. swept the floor
15. fond of candy
16. silly
17. the poem about love
18. read the poem about love
19. jumped over the barn
20. saw those kids

---

### REMINDER

Use the substitution test to help you determine the type of phrase you are dealing with. The substitution test not only tells you if a group of words is or is not a phrase, but also can tell you the type of phrase you have. So . . . don't just guess.

---

## SUBCATEGORIZATION (Section 2, pp. 196–202)

Phrase structure rules provide the structure for a sentence. To make the sentence grammatical, words must be inserted into the structure generated by the phrase structure rules. And since we only want to generate the grammatical sentences of a language, there must be restrictions on how words are inserted into a sentence's structure. Two of these restrictions are outlined below.

- **Lexical category.** One obvious restriction is that the lexical category of the word must match the lexical category into which it is being inserted. For example, verbs can only be inserted into a verb node, nouns into a noun node, adjectives into an adjective node, etc.

- **Complement options.** A second restriction is that the word's complement option must match the complement structure generated by the phrase structure rules. For example, many verbs (e.g., *throw*) require a complement noun phrase and therefore must be inserted into a structure containing a noun phrase in the complement position. If such a verb were entered into a structure without a noun phrase complement, the result would be an ungrammatical sentence.

Information on the lexical category and complement options of words along with information on their meaning and pronunciation are found in a speaker's mental lexicon. Complement options are often referred to as subcategorization.

## Practice 5.6: Subcategorization

1. Determine the complement options that the verbs listed below require. Do this by thinking of grammatical and ungrammatical sentences containing the verb.

   |   |   |
   |---|---|
   | 1. panic | 4. write |
   | 2. watch | 5. wonder |
   | 3. imagine | 6. play |

2. Nouns, adjectives, and prepositions also have restrictions on the types of complements with which they can and cannot occur. Determine the complement options required by the following lexical items.

   |   |   |
   |---|---|
   | 1. pleasure | 4. intelligent |
   | 2. with | 5. at |
   | 3. contribution | 6. upset |

## SIMPLE SENTENCES (Section 1.3, pp. 192–193)

If phrases consist of categories, then it follows that sentences consist of phrases. A sentence consists of three elements:

- **NP.** This noun phrase is typically referred to as the subject and can consist of any of the possibilities we saw during our discussion of phrases. The subject is often considered to be the specifier of I.

- **I (Infl).** This is the head of the sentence, and is used to refer to inflection. There are two possibilities for I: +Pst and –Pst. +Pst is used for sentences in the past tense, and –Pst is used for sentences in either the present or future.

- **VP.** The verb phrase is a part of what is typically referred to as the predicate. Like the subject NP, the VP can consist of any of the possibilities we saw during our discussion of phrases. The VP is often considered to function as the complement of I.

If the sentence is considered to be IP (Inflection Phrase), then the internal structure is consistent with the phrase structure schema: IP consists of a specifier (NP), a head (I), and a complement (VP).

The two different types of sentences we will focus on are:

- simple sentences
- sentences with complement clauses

## Simple Sentences

A simple sentence consists of an NP, I, and a VP, and can be diagrammed as follows.

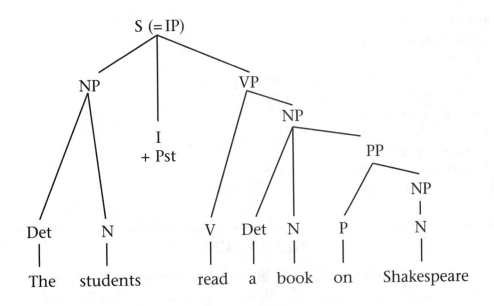

A simple sentence may optionally contain an auxiliary verb. An auxiliary verb occupies the I position. Such sentences can be diagrammed as follows.

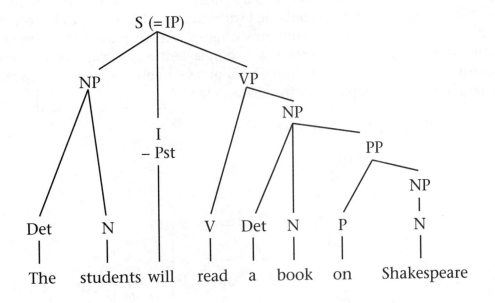

## PRACTICE 5.7: Diagramming simple sentences

The following exercise will give you some practice with simple sentences. Draw a tree diagram for each of the following sentences.

1. Students often write exams.
2. A penguin walked into the room.
3. Dogs should always go for a walk.
4. Those monsters may hide under the bed.
5. Abner concealed the document.
6. Marge usually watches the sunset.
7. The children often play with a dinosaur.
8. That garbage smells.
9. Grandparents may live in condominiums.
10. Doctors care about people.

---

### REMINDER

Construct your tree diagrams above the sentence, not below it!

---

## SENTENCES WITH COMPLEMENT CLAUSES
(Section 2.3, pp. 200–202)

Sentences themselves may also function as complements. That is, sentences can occur within phrases. These sentences that are contained within larger phrases are called complement clauses (CP). A clause is a syntactic unit consisting of a noun phrase and a verb phrase. Complement clauses are typically preceded by a complementizer such as *that, if,* and *whether.* A complement clause may be found within a verb phrase, noun phrase, adjective phrase, or prepositional phrase. An example of each is given below:

1. **VP:** John [VPbelieves [CPthat the world is round]].

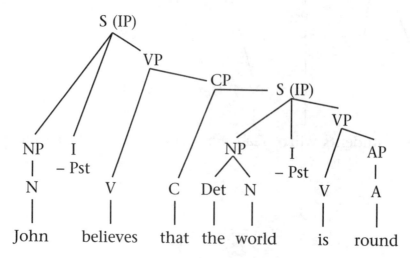

2. **NP:** John believes [<sub>NP</sub>the claim [<sub>CP</sub>that the world is round]].

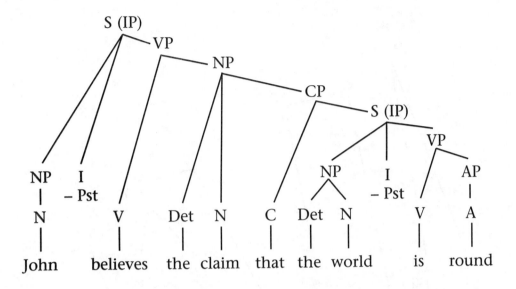

3. **AP:** John is [<sub>AP</sub>satisfied [<sub>CP</sub>that the world is round]].

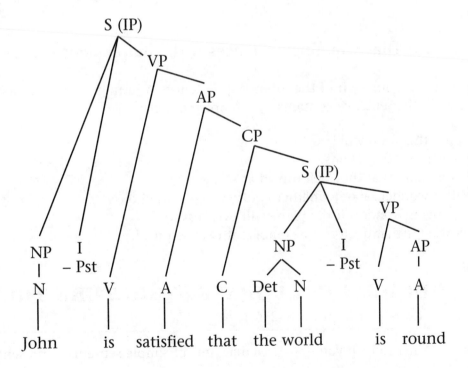

4. **PP:** John wondered [<sub>PP</sub>about [<sub>CP</sub>whether the world is round]].

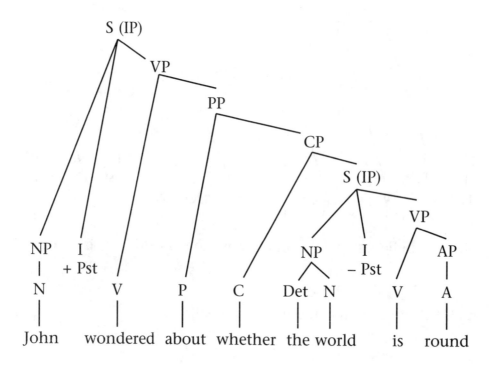

## PRACTICE 5.8: Diagramming sentences with complement clauses

Draw a tree diagram for each of the following sentences. You might want to first determine which phrase of the sentence contains the complement clause.

1. Stan hopes that Sean will become a pilot.
2. Nancy has proof that aliens exist.
3. Sailors are afraid that they will drown at sea.
4. The realtor wonders about whether Louise will sell the house.
5. The passengers wonders if the plane will ever leave.
6. The knowledge that doctors are competent is widespread.

## HINTS FOR DRAWING PHRASE STRUCTURE TREES
(See Appendix to Chapter 5, pp. 233–236.)

Here are some hints to help you draw tree diagrams of simple sentences and sentences with complement clauses.

1. Determine whether the sentence is simple or contains a complement clause. A good clue that a sentence contains a complement clause is the presence of a complementizer such as *that, if,* or *whether.*

2. If a sentence contains a complement clause, diagram this clause first. Remember that a complement clause consists of a complementizer followed by a sentence (usually, but not always, simple).

3. A simple sentence consists of an NP, I, and a VP. Start by identifying the main verb of the sentence. Check if this verb has a qualifier and/or a complement. Remember that the qualifier marks the beginning of the phrase, and the complement, the end. Diagram the verb phrase.

4. Next, determine I. Remember that I can be either –Pst or +Pst. +Pst is only used if a sentence is in the past tense. Auxiliary verbs such as *may, will,* or *should* occur under I.

5. Diagram the subject NP. Remember that an optional determiner marks the beginning of the noun phrase, and either the noun or a complement marks the end of the noun phrase.

6. If the sentence just diagrammed is part of a complement clause, then diagram the CP. Remember that the CP will consist of the complementizer plus the sentence just diagrammed. Then complete the phrase containing the CP and the rest of the sentence, just as you would for any simple sentence (as above).

## PRACTICE 5.9: More practice with phrase structure trees

The following exercise contains many examples of simple sentences as well as sentences with complement clauses. Draw a tree diagram for each. Watch out, they get harder.

1. Neighbors can be unfriendly.
2. The train for Princeton left.
3. That soup tastes really great.
4. The repairman fixed the watch.
5. Children are curious about everything.
6. Animals sometimes become very ill.
7. Kitty was very glad that Red won the car.
8. The tourists hope that they might see a whale.
9. Nurses never complain about the fact that they are caregivers.
10. The salesman wonders if those customers will buy the car.

# MODEL OF THE GRAMMAR
(Section 1.2, pp. 187–191; Sections 3.1–3.3, pp. 203–213)

---

The syntactic component of the grammar is organized as follows:

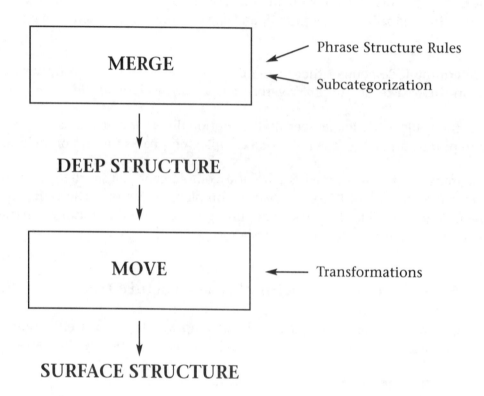

Two operations may be involved in sequence:

1. **Merge.** The Merge operation is responsible for building the sentences of a language. The Merge operation combines heads with specifiers and complements according to the phrase structure rules of the language and the complement options required by the head. The phrase structure rules along with subcategorization create a deep structure representation of a sentence.

2. **Move.** The Move operation moves elements in the deep structure to create the surface structure. The surface structure is sometimes called the final syntactic form. Movement is optional. If no movement occurs, the deep and surface structure is the same. If movement occurs, then the deep and surface structure are no longer the same. Movements are historically called transformations because they served to transform one sentence type into another (e.g., a statement into a question).

The following pages will emphasize different types of transformations.

# TRANSFORMATIONS (Sections 3.1–3.3, pp. 202–213)

Transformations (Move operations) move elements of the deep structure to create the surface structure. These movements manipulate the deep structure to create other sentence types such as questions.

Four transformations will be considered:

- Inversion
- *Wh* Movement
- *Do* Insertion
- NP Movement

## INVERSION AND *Wh* MOVEMENT

Transformations are often used to create questions. Two common types of questions are *yes-no* questions and *wh* questions. *Yes-no* questions are so named because the response is usually yes or no. *Wh* questions are so named because they begin with a *wh* question word (e.g., *what*). *Yes-no* questions are the result of a transformation called Inversion, while *wh* questions are the result of *Wh* Movement and Inversion. Informal versions of these two transformations are given below.

**Inversion:**         Inversion moves the auxiliary verb to the left of the subject NP
              e.g., George *should* phone home. ———→
                          *Should* George phone home?

**Wh Movement:**     *Wh* Movement moves a *wh* phrase to the beginning of the sentence.
              e.g., George *should* phone home *when* ———→
                          *Should* George phone home *when* ———→
                          *When should* George phone home?

## *Do* INSERTION

Auxiliary verbs are optional in English. Therefore, there are many English sentences that do not contain auxiliary verbs. Yet, these sentences can still be transformed into questions. This is done by inserting *do, did,* or *does* into the sentence, which then gets inverted. The form of *do* used depends on the tense of the sentence. *Do* Insertion is often needed for both *yes-no* and *wh* questions.

This transformation can be stated informally as:

**Do Insertion:**      Insert *do* as the auxiliary verb of the sentence.
              e.g., George phoned home. ———→
                          George *did* phone home ———→
                          *Did* George phone home?

e.g., George phoned home *when* ⟶

George *did* phone home *when* ⟶

*Did* George phone home *when* ⟶

*When did* George phone home?

## PRACTICE 5.10: Inversion, *Wh* Movement, and *Do* Insertion

For each of the following questions, list all the transformations that have been applied to create it. It might help to first identify the type of question (*yes-no* or *wh*). Remember that more than one transformation can occur.

1. Will the trip be fun?

_____

2. What should George buy for his mother?

_____

3. Does Gillian like fish?

_____

4. Whom did David fire?

_____

5. Can the dog stay at your house?

_____

## NP MOVEMENT

In addition to the three preceding transformations, other structures such as passives have often been analyzed as resulting from the application of transformations. Consider the following example:

The workers broke the machine.
The machine was broken by the workers.

The first is an active sentence, and the second, a passive sentence. Note that both sentences convey the identical meaning. In an active sentence, the subject NP (*the workers*) is the agent (doer of the action), while in a passive sentence, the theme (entity undergoing the action) is in the subject position (*the machine*).

In many theories of grammar, passive sentences are analyzed as the result of a transformation that operates on a deep structure in which the subject has been demoted to a less prominent position. This transformation can be formulated as follows:

**NP Movement:**   Move NP into the subject position.

e.g., (empty subject) was broken *the machine* by the workers

⟶ *The machine* was broken by the workers.

NP Movement moves the theme into the empty subject position resulting in a passive sentence.

**Remember:** NP movement can interact with the other transformations discussed. Consider, for example, the sentence with the following deep structure:

| | |
|---|---|
| **Deep:** | (empty subject) *was* broken *the machine* by the workers. |
| **NP Movement:** | *The machine was* broken by the workers. |
| **Inversion:** | *Was the machine* broken by the workers? |
| **Surface:** | *Was the machine* broken by the workers? |

In the above sentence, NP movement is applied to create a passive sentence. Inversion is then applied to create a *yes-no* question. The surface structure, therefore, is both a passive sentence and a *yes-no* question.

# IDENTIFYING DEEP STRUCTURE AND TRANSFORMATIONS (Section 3.3, pp. 211–212)

You need to be able to determine the deep structure for any sentence you are given and to identify any of the transformations (including NP Movement) that have occurred. You may also have to construct a tree diagram of the deep structure.

Here are some clues to help you identify transformations and put surface structure sentences back into deep structure:

| YOU SEE: | YOU THINK: | YOU DO: |
|---|---|---|
| The auxiliary verb before the subject. A *yes-no* question. | Inversion has taken place. | Put the auxiliary back to its deep structure position after the subject NP. |
| A *wh* word or phrase. | *Wh* Movement has taken place. | Examine each verb in the sentence. Determine which verb is missing either a subject or an object, and put the *wh* word or phrase into that position. |

| YOU SEE: | YOU THINK: | YOU DO: |
|---|---|---|
| *Do, Did,* or *Does* at the beginning of a sentence or after a *Wh* phrase. | *Do* Insertion has taken place. | Remove *do, did,* or *does* from the sentence. |
| A sentence in which the subject NP is not the agent (doer) of the action. | NP Movement has taken place. | Move the subject NP back to its deep structure position after the main verb. |

## PRACTICE 5.11: Deep structure and transformations

For each of the following surface structure sentences, determine the deep structure, list the transformations that were used to create the surface structure, and provide a tree diagram of the deep structure.

1. Will the plane leave on time?
2. What did you paint?
3. Did George faint at the bus station?
4. Jessica was invited by the queen.
5. Was the floor swept by elves?

## PRACTICE 5.12: Practice with transformations
(Sections 2–3, pp. 196–214)

Determine and draw a tree diagram of the deep structure of each of the following sentences, and list any and all transformations that occurred to derive the surface structure.

1. Must the musicians play that music?
2. Who does the jury blame?
3. Margo thinks that Frances might fly the plane to England.
4. Did the staff throw a party for Sam?
5. Was the billboard destroyed by vandals?
6. Colin thinks that girls never phone George.
7. Who will those new immigrants live with?
8. Barry said that the meal was prepared by the chef.
9. Which box are the dishes in?
10. Will the winner claim the prize?
11. Pat knows that Chris would like the meal.
12. Do children like cake?

---

**REMINDERS**

1. You are trying to determine which transformations have already been applied; therefore, you must *never* apply any additional transformations.
2. No transformations need apply, only one transformation may apply, or more than one transformation may apply.

---

# UNIVERSAL GRAMMAR AND VARIATION (Section 4, pp. 214–221)

Our focus so far has been on English sentence structure; however, just as we have seen with phonetics, phonology, and morphology, there is much syntactic variation across languages. There are three main types of variation: variation in syntactic categories, variation in phrase structure rules, and variation in transformations.

- **Syntactic categories.** Nouns, verbs, adjectives, and prepositions are all found in English; however, only nouns and verbs are found in all languages. Many languages lack adjectives, and some even lack both adjectives and prepositions.

- **Phrase structure rules.** English is a head-medial language, meaning that specifiers come before the head and complements after the head; however, this is not true of all languages. In many languages (e.g., Thai), the head comes before the specifier and complement (head-initial), and in others (e.g., Japanese), the head comes after the specifier and complement (head-final).

- **Transformations.** While English uses Inversion and *Wh* Movement to create questions, this is not true of all languages. Many languages (e.g., Tamil) create *yes-no* questions using a question morpheme, and in many languages (e.g., Korean, Chinese, Japanese, Thai), *wh* words are not moved to the beginning of a sentence but are left in their deep structure position. In addition, there are other transformations (e.g., verb raising) that are not normally found in English but can be found in languages such as French.

All of the variation discussed above is only superficial. Languages have many common properties. *Universal Grammar (UG)* is the system of categories, operations, and principles shared by all languages. These operations include the Merge and Move operations discussed as well as the mental lexicon, which contains information about the pronunciation, form, and meaning of the words in a language. UG also allows for variation, which is captured using *parameters*. For example, a head-position parameter captures the three possibilities for assembling sentences: head-initial, head-medial, and head-final. Languages select one of these settings, and different languages often select different settings.

## PRACTICE 5.13: Transformations and phrase structure in other languages

1. Examine the following hypothetical language data and determine how *yes-no* and *wh* questions are constructed in this language. How are these different from English? Suggest a parameter that might capture the differences between this language and English.

   a.  gurus-us       e       orbu   tebe   pa  
       children      might  see    goat   QUESTION  
       Might the children see the goat?

   b.  gurus-us       e       orbu  bu  
       children      might  see    what  
       What might the children see?

2. Now, examine the following Japanese data and construct a set of phrase structure rules for the language. You will need a rule for S, NP, VP, and PP. How do these phrase structure rules differ from English? Does this language have prepositions (which come before a complement NP) or postpositions (which come after a complement NP)?

   a.  Taroo-ga son gakusei-o hihansita  
      Taroo   the    student    criticized  
      Taroo criticized the student.

   b.  Sono syoonen-ga isu   ni    suwatta  
      the    boy     chair   on    sat  
      The boy sat on the chair.

   c.  Hanako-ga ho-o    tukue no oita  
      Hanako   book   table   on   put  
      Hanako put the book on the table.

---

## REVIEW: IMPORTANT TERMS

Following are some important syntactic terms from the chapter that you should know.

- active
- categories
- clause
- complements
- deep structure
- head

- Merge operation
- movement test
- particle
- passive
- phrase structure
- specifiers

- subcategorization
- substitution test
- surface structure
- transformation (Move)
- *wh* questions
- *yes-no* questions

# REVIEW EXERCISE

Draw a tree diagram for each of the following sentences. You will need to use what you have learned about simple sentences, sentences with complement clauses, and various types of transformations. If transformations have applied, draw the deep structure and list the transformations.

1. Sally lives in a house by the sea.
2. The unicorn might eat the lilies.
3. The rabbit hid under the bridge.
4. The castle fell into the sea.
5. The governors seem certain that the candidate will win the election.
6. Did Bill sell that house?
7. Does William think that Harry can survive in the jungle?
8. The jury believed that the prisoner was guilty.
9. The little boy was frightened by the clown.
10. What does Mary want for Christmas?

☑ **RECAP**

If you can do the following, then you've conquered syntax. (See also the Key Terms on pp. 231–232 of the main text.)

- describe the differences between lexical and nonlexical **categories**
- assign words to their syntactic category
- determine whether a group of words is a phrase
- identify and diagram phrases
- diagram simple sentences and complement clause **structures**
- understand phrase structure rules
- understand how the Merge operation builds sentences
- determine complement options
- find the deep structure of a sentence
- spot transformations (Move operations)
- analyze non-English language data

## QUESTIONS? PROBLEMS?

# six

# SEMANTICS: THE ANALYSIS OF MEANING

Semantics is the study of meaning in human language. Both words and sentences have meaning; however, the meaning of a sentence goes beyond the meaning of the individual words making up the sentence. As we shall see, meaning, particularly the meaning of words, is very difficult to determine.

Following are some of the important concepts and topics covered in this chapter. Make sure you are familiar with them.

Meaning
Concepts
Semantic relations
Ambiguity
Thematic roles
Other factors in sentence interpretation
Conversation

## MEANING (Section 1, pp. 246–253)

As native speakers of a language, we all know the meaning of a great many words in our language. And if we come across a word whose meaning is unknown to us, we can always look it up in a dictionary. But, to understand the dictionary definition, we need to understand the meanings of the words making up the definition. While no definitive theory of meaning exists, some possibilities include connotation, denotation, extension and intension, and componential analysis.

### Connotation

This theory states that the meaning of a word is simply the set of associations that the word evokes. For example, *winter* could be taken to mean a cold, dreary, snowy time of year. The main problem with this theory is that many words evoke different associations for different people.

### Denotation

This theory states that the meaning of a word is not the set of associations it evokes, but rather the referent of the word. Accordingly then, *winter* would simply refer to a particular time of year. However, there are many words (e.g., *unicorn*), that have no referent.

## Extension and Intension

This theory attempts to combine the first two. Extension refers to the referent of a word, and intension to the associations it evokes. In reference to the example of *winter,* the extension is the particular time of year that *winter* refers to, and the intension is that *winter* is cold, dreary, and snowy (at least for some). Thus, the meaning of a word includes both its extension and its intension.

## Componential Analysis

This theory is based on the idea that meaning can be decomposed into smaller units in the same way that sounds can be decomposed into the properties making them up. These individual properties of sounds and meaning are called features. Different combinations of phonetic features create different sounds. For example, the phonetic features [+consonantal, –syllabic, –sonorant, –continuant] give us the natural class of stops. Semantic features can be combined in a similar fashion. For example, the semantic features [+living, –human, –adult] give us the category of baby animals. Adding additional features gives us a more specific type of baby animal. For example, adding [+canine] to the above matrix results in the "puppy" category of baby animals. This type of analysis allows us to capture similarities and differences between words. But, can all meaning be broken down into smaller units?

## PRACTICE 6.1: Theories of meaning

1.  For each of the following expressions, attempt to define its meaning according to the theories of connotation, denotation, and extension and intension discussed above.

    a.  summer
    b.  a linguistics instructor
    c.  grass

2.  Examine the following two groups of words and determine the semantic feature(s) each group has in common. What semantic feature(s) are different among members of each group? What about between the two groups?

    Group A: grandmother / mother / daughter / widow
    Group B: grandfather / father / son / widower

3.  Now try doing a componential analysis for:  • ewe and lamb
                                                  • mare, filly, and colt

## CONCEPTS (Section 2, pp. 253–261)

While much remains unknown about the nature of meaning and how it is represented in our minds, we all use words and sentences to express meaning, and we do this very successfully. Linguists use the term *concepts* to refer to the system we use to identify, classify, and organize all elements of our many and varied experiences.

## Fuzzy Concepts

Fuzzy concepts are concepts that can differ from person to person. They have no specific referent. For example, whether something is expensive or not is relative. For some, an item costing $5.00 is expensive, while for others, something may not be expensive until it costs $5,000.

## Graded Membership

Concepts can be organized according to how typical they are within a particular category. We select one member as the prototype. This member is considered the most typical within the category. Other members are arranged around the prototype, with members closer to the prototype sharing more properties and members farther from the prototype sharing fewer properties.

## Metaphor

The concepts expressed by language do not exist in isolation but are interconnected and associated. Metaphors—the understanding of one concept in terms of another—can be used to make these connections. For example, time is often referred to as a commodity that can be saved (e.g., This device will save you hours of time) or wasted (e.g., This meeting is a waste of time). Other examples include comparing emotions to spatial terms such as *up* or *down* (e.g., George is feeling down today) or even attributing animal-like properties to people (e.g., Mary is as gentle as a lamb).

## Lexicalization

Lexicalization refers to the process whereby concepts are encoded into the meanings of words. How concepts are encoded varies from language to language. For example, in English, many verbs such as *roll, slide,* and *limp* contain both the idea of motion as well as the manner in which the motion occurs. Other languages (e.g., Spanish) cannot use one word to express both concepts, but require separate words for each. Still other languages (e.g., Atsugewi—an Amerindian language) use one word to express both motion and the type of object that moves.

## Grammaticization

Grammaticization refers to concepts that are expressed as affixes or functional categories. For example, in English, the distinction between singular and plural is expressed as an affix. It has been grammaticized. Concepts such as tense, number, and negation are often grammaticized across languages. However, many other concepts can also be grammaticized. For example, color adjectives in Classical Arabic are marked for whether they indicate a primary or secondary color.

## PRACTICE 6.2: Concepts

1. For each of the following concepts, determine whether they are fuzzy, are graded, or have been grammaticized.

a. the comparative and superlative
b. cats
c. mountains
d. time
e. vegetables

For any of the above that exhibit a graded membership, determine the member that is prototypical for you. How might this differ from person to person?

2. **Cree.** Quite often languages contain different forms of grammaticized affixes or functional categories whose use depends on some semantic characteristic of a stem or complement. Consider the data below from Cree involving possession and answer the questions that follow.

| | Unpossessed Noun | Gloss | Possessed Noun | Gloss |
|---|---|---|---|---|
| 1. | *spiton | 'an arm' | nispiton | 'my arm' |
| 2. | *skiːsik | 'an eye' | niskiːsik | 'my eye' |
| 3. | *htawiya | 'a father' | noːhtawiya | 'my father' |
| 4. | *kaːwiya | 'a mother' | noːkaːwiya | 'my mother' |
| 5. | tʃimaːn | 'a canoe' | nitʃimaːn | 'my canoe' |
| 6. | astotin | 'a cap' | nitastotin | 'my cap' |

Why is it wrong to have the words in 1–4 in the unpossessed form in Cree? What is the semantic basis for this? Think about which of the above you could give away and which you could not give away.

3. **Swahili.** The language data below illustrate differences in the use of singular and plural prefixes in Swahili. Group the nouns into classes based on their use of the different prefixes. What is the semantic basis for your grouping?

| | Singular | Plural | Gloss |
|---|---|---|---|
| 1. | mtoto | watoto | 'child' |
| 2. | mhindi | mihindi | 'corn' |
| 3. | kikombe | vikombe | 'hair' |
| 4. | mkindu | mikindu | 'date palm' |
| 5. | mfigili | mifigili | 'radish' |
| 6. | mwalimu | wawalimu | 'teacher' |
| 7. | kioo | vioo | 'mirror' |
| 8. | mume | waume | 'husband' |
| 9. | kikapu | vikapu | 'basket' |
| 10. | mboga | miboga | 'pumpkin' |

4. **German.** German neuter nouns can occur in a prepositional phrase either in the dative case (definite article *dem*) or in the accusative case (definite article *das*). Examine the following sentences and determine the semantic basis for the choice of either the dative or the accusative case.

1.  *Monika arbeitet in dem Kaffeehaus.* 'Monika works in the coffeehouse.'
    *Stefan kommt in das Kaffeehaus.* 'Stefan comes into the coffeehouse.'

2.  *Ritas Stuhl steht neben dem Fenster.* 'Rita's chair stands next to the window.'
    *Jan stellt seinen Stuhl neben das Fenster.* 'Jan puts his chair next to the window.'

3.  *Ein Schuh steht unter dem Bett.* 'A shoe is under the bed.'
    *Kurt stellt den anderen Schuh unter das Bett.* 'Kurt puts the other shoe under the bed.'

4.  *Ilsa ist in dem Wohnzimmer.* 'Ilsa is in the living room.'
    *Armin geht in das Wohnzimmer.* 'Armin goes into the living room.'

How is German different from English? What concept is contained in the German articles that is not found in English articles?

## SEMANTIC RELATIONS (Sections 1.1–1.2, pp. 246–249)

While it is very difficult to determine the meanings of words and how they are represented in our minds, it is much easier to define and spot the relations that exist between words as well as between sentences.

**Relations between words:**

*   Synonyms—two words that have similar meanings
        e.g., filbert / hazelnut

*   Antonyms—two words that have opposite meanings
        e.g., hot / cold

*   Homonyms (polysemy)—one word that has two or more related meanings
        e.g., bright (shining or intelligent)

*   Homophones—two words with the same form (i.e., pronunciation) but two distinct meanings
            e.g., pen (a writing instrument or an enclosure)

**Relations between sentences:**

*   Paraphrases—two sentences that have different forms but the same meaning
            e.g., The cat ate the mouse.
                The mouse was eaten by the cat.

*   Contradiction—two sentences such that if one is true, the second must be false
            e.g., George is rich.
                George can't afford ground beef.

*   Entailment—two sentences in which the truth of the first implies the truth of the second, but the truth of the second does not necessarily imply the truth of the first.
            e.g., George killed the burglar.
                The burglar is dead.

## PRACTICE 6.3: Identifying semantic relations

For each of the following, identify the relation that exists between either the words or the sentences. The first one is done for you.

1. test
   exam                                        _____synonyms_____

2. Mary sang a solo.
   The solo was sung by Mary.                  _____

3. bug (insect)
   bug (microphone)                            _____

4. Sam is a widower.
   Sam's wife is alive.                        _____

5. The shark bit a swimmer.
   The swimmer is injured.                     _____

6. parent
   offspring                                   _____

7. George gave Sally the book.
   George gave a book to Sally.                _____

8. Nancy prepared salmon for dinner.
   There is nothing to eat for dinner.         _____

9. hungry
   famished                                    _____

10. steak (a piece of meat)
    stake (a sharp piece of wood)              _____

---

## REMINDER

Homonyms and homophones are not the same. Homonyms have related meanings while homophones have unrelated meanings.

## AMBIGUITY (Section 1.1, pp. 246–248; Section 3.2, pp. 263–264)

A sentence is ambiguous when it has more than one meaning. There are two main types of ambiguity, as outlined below.

- **Lexical ambiguity.** This type of ambiguity results from one word in the sentence having more than one meaning. Polysemy and homophony give us lexical ambiguity. For example, the sentence *The glasses are on the table* has two meanings: (1) the drinking glasses are on the table, and (2) the eyeglasses are on the table. The ambiguity arises because the word *glasses* has two possible meanings.

- **Structural ambiguity.** This type of ambiguity results from a phrase in the sentence having more than one possible structure. Each possible structure is associated with a different meaning.

Consider the ambiguous sentence *The surface was painted with red flowers and leaves*. In this sentence, the ambiguity is found within the noun phrase, which will, therefore, have two different syntactic structures.

**Meaning One:**     Both the flowers and the leaves are red.

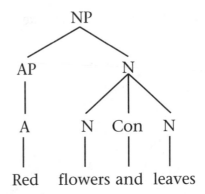

**Meaning Two:**     Only the flowers are red.

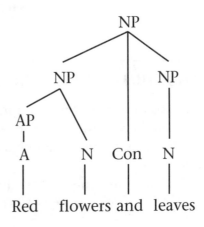

Ambiguity can also be found within the verb phrase. Consider the ambiguous sentence *Sam ate the cake in the kitchen.* In this example, the verb phrase has two different possible structures.

**Meaning One:**     Sam ate the cake that was in the kitchen.

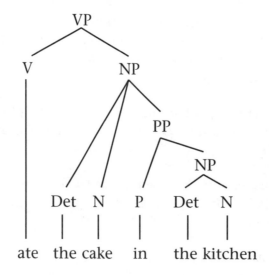

**Meaning Two:**     Sam was in the kitchen eating cake.

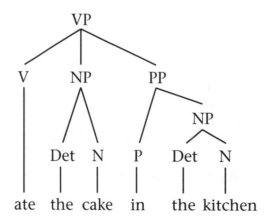

---

### SOME HINTS FOR IDENTIFYING AMBIGUITY

1.  Determine if the ambiguity is coming from one word in the sentence (lexical) or from more than one possible combination of the words in the sentence (structural).
2.  For lexical ambiguity, identify the word that is ambiguous and determine the two (or more) possible meanings of the word.
3.  For structural ambiguity, determine the phrase containing the ambiguity (usually noun or verb) and the possible meanings. Match each meaning with a different syntactic structure.

## PRACTICE 6.4: Identifying ambiguity

Each of the following sentences is ambiguous. For each sentence, state whether the ambiguity is lexical or structural and provide an unambiguous phrase or sentence for each possible meaning.

1. Cool beer and wine are what we want.
2. I met the woman standing by the water cooler.
3. Congress passed a dangerous drug bill.
4. Businessmen like black and white ties.
5. George and Harry or Fred will draw the picture.
6. I want to look at the pictures in the attic.
7. The instructor left his key in the office.

Draw tree structures for ambiguous phrases in nos. 1, 3, 5, and 6. Remember that each meaning will have a different structure.

## THEMATIC ROLES (Section 3.3, pp. 264–268)

As we have seen, the structure of a sentence is very closely related to the meaning of that sentence. Different structures give rise to different meanings. Another important element of sentence interpretation involves the roles that are assigned to the noun phrases within a sentence. That is, to interpret any sentence, we need to know who the actor of the action is, what is undergoing the action, the location of the action, the instrument used in the action, etc. These roles that are assigned to the noun phrases within a sentence are called the thematic, or theta, roles.

There are three important properties of thematic roles.

- **Common thematic roles.**  Some of the common thematic roles include:

  Agent (actor)—The entity performing an action.
  Theme—The entity undergoing an action.
  Source—The starting point of a movement.
  Goal—The end point of a movement.
  Location—The place where an action occurs.
  Instrument—The entity used to perform an action.

- **Thematic role assignment.**  Thematic roles are assigned to noun phrases based on their position within the sentence. Typically, verbs and prepositions assign thematic roles.

  | Verbs | Assign the agent role (if it has one) to its subject noun phrase |
  | | Assign the theme role (if it has one) to its complement noun phrase |

  | Prepositions | Assign a thematic role (the specific one depends on the preposition) to its complement noun phrase |

  Knowledge of the thematic roles that verbs and prepositions assign is stored in our mental lexicon.

Thematic role assignment can be diagrammed as follows:

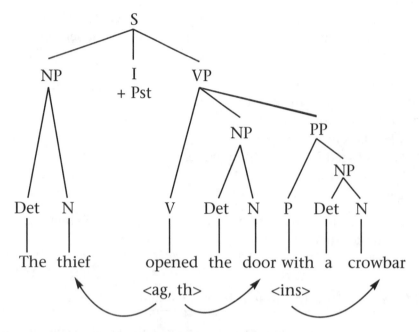

In the above sentence, the verb *open* assigns the agent role <ag> to the noun phrase *the thief* and the theme role <th> to the noun phrase *the door,* while the preposition *with* assigns the instrument role <ins> to its complement noun phrase *a crowbar*.

• **Thematic roles and deep structure.** Thematic roles are assigned at deep structure. Recall from syntax that deep structure is the result of the Merge operation. For sentences in which noun phrases have been moved from their initial position, they must be moved back to this position to determine the verb/preposition that has assigned its thematic role. For example, the *wh* question, *What did George lose?* has the deep structure *George lost what.* Accordingly, the verb *lost* assigns the agent role to George and the theme role to *what. What* retains this role even after it is moved.

## PRACTICE 6.5: Identifying thematic roles

For each of the following sentences, identify all the noun phrases and the thematic role assigned to each noun phrase.

1. Sarah drove that bus from Indianapolis to Terre Haute.
2. The children are eating their ice cream with spoons.
3. Which shoes did you buy at the store?
4. The cat was chased around the garden by a large dog.
5. The boys walked to the park.
6. Sally mailed her nephew a parcel.
7. What did Bill leave at your house?
8. The letter was sent.
9. Ginger scribbled her address on the paper with a pen.
10. The minister in the pulpit was ordained recently.

Go back through each sentence and for each thematic role, determine the verb or preposition that assigned the role. Make sure you put any sentences in which a transformation has occurred into deep structure first.

# OTHER FACTORS IN SENTENCE INTERPRETATION
(Section 4, pp. 271–277)

Besides the structure of a sentence and the thematic roles assigned to the noun phrases within a sentence, there are many other factors involved in sentence interpretation. These include the beliefs and attitudes of the speaker, the setting in which the sentence occurs, the topic of the sentence, and many more.

*Pragmatics* is the study of the role of these factors in sentence interpretation.

### Beliefs and Attitudes

Nonlinguistic knowledge can be used to interpret elements within a sentence. For example, in the sentence *The city council denied the demonstrators a permit because they advocated violence,* we assume that the pronoun *they* refers to the demonstrators and not the council members because of our beliefs about demonstrators. If we change the verb from *advocate* to *abhor,* we now assume that *they* refers to the council and not the demonstrators. Again, this is based on our world beliefs.

### Presupposition

Presupposition refers to the assumption or belief implied by the use of a particular word. For example, in the sentence *John admitted that the soccer team had won the game,* the use of the verb *admit* presupposes or implies that the team had actually won. A similar implication is not present in the sentence *John said that the soccer team had won the game.*

### Setting/Deictics

The form and interpretation of some words depends on the location of the speaker and listener within a particular setting. These words are called deictics. Some examples of English deictics include *here/there* and *this/that. Here* and *this* are used to refer to items close to the speaker, while *there* and *that* are used to refer to words close to the listener.

### Discourse

Many sentences can only be interpreted in reference to information contained in preceding sentences. Discourse is the term used to describe the connected series of utterances that are produced during a conversation, lecture, story, or other type of speech act. Old (given) information refers to knowledge that is known to the participants of the speech act, while new information refers to knowledge that is introduced into the speech act for the first time. In addition, many languages (e.g., Japanese) use a marker to indicate the topic of the discourse.

## PRACTICE 6.6: Sentence interpretation

Sentences can be difficult to interpret because they are ungrammatical, because they violate our knowledge of the world, or because they contain words that have no known referent. Identify why each of the following sentences is hard to interpret.

1. Our ten-month-old son is six feet tall.
2. Mike red bought car a.
3. Palm trees grow vigorously at the North Pole.
4. Radiculus glautons are found in the soil.
5. The bumblebee picked up the cat and flew back to the hive with it.

• Go back and reconsider sentence 4. What meaning might you assign to the unknown words in this sentence? What about the meaning of the overall sentence?

• Why might the sentence *His mother wants you to be a doctor* be difficult to interpret as a stand-alone sentence (i.e., not as part of a discourse)?

## CONVERSATION (Section 4.4, pp. 275–277)

Not only do words and sentences have meaning, but they also are used to convey messages. We often do this by having a conversation with someone. To have a successful conversation, there are rules that must be followed. H. P. Grice proposed a number of conversational principles and maxims.

• **General principle.** The general principle guiding all conversational interactions is the Cooperative Principle.

  **Cooperative Principle**—Make your contribution appropriate to the conversation.

• **Specific maxims.** Grice also proposed more specific guidelines (i.e., maxims) for conversation. If we follow these maxims, then we have adhered to the Cooperative Principle and can successfully use the meanings found in language to convey information. Four of these maxims are presented below.

  **Maxim of Relation**—Make your contribution relevant to the conversation.

  **Maxim of Quality**—Make your contribution truthful.

  **Maxim of Quantity**—Make your contribution only as informative as required.

  **Maxim of Manner**—Make your contribution unambiguous, clear, and logical.

• **Conversational implicature.** During the course of a conversation, we are often able to make inferences about what is meant but was not actually said. Consider, for example, the following interaction:

  Mike: How did you do on the last exam?
  Jim: Want to come with me to the Registrar's Office?

In the above example, Jim violates the Maxim of Relation, and even though he doesn't actually say how he did on the exam, it can be inferred from his response that he did rather badly.

## PRACTICE 6.7: Violations of conversational maxims

You've just missed your bus and are standing at the bus stop waiting for the next one. The time is 2 P.M. and the next bus is due at 2:15 P.M., but you don't know that. You ask someone at the bus stop when the next bus is due, and receive several replies. Each reply you receive may or may not violate one or more of Grice's conversational maxims. For each reply, identify which maxim(s), if any, have been violated.

1. When's the next bus?
   At 2:30. (He's lying.)

   _____

2. When's the next bus?
   When I was little, I was obsessed with buses. I wanted to be a bus driver. I had hundreds of different kinds of buses. Little buses, big buses, red buses, blue buses, and even double-deckered buses. Did you know that in England, many buses are double-deckered? I have made a study of buses. I think the next bus will be here in 15 minutes. Did you know that in India there are no buses? Did you know I wanted to be a bus driver? Did you know . . .

   _____

3. When's the next bus?
   Let me think! If the last bus was here at 1:50 and if they run every 20 minutes or so, then the next bus should be here at 2:10. (He has no idea.)

   _____

4. When's the next bus?
   At 2:15, but if we were in Denver that would be 3:15.

   _____

5. When's the next bus?
   I don't know.

   _____

# REVIEW EXERCISES

1. **Grammaticized concepts:** Look at the data from Burmese. What concept is grammaticized in Burmese that is usually not grammaticized in English? How is this concept indicated?

   [ ̥] below a sound indicates that it is voiceless.
   Tones are marked as diacritics above the vowels.

   |   |       |               |       |              |
   |---|-------|---------------|-------|--------------|
   | 1. | mjô  | 'be floating' | m̥jô  | 'set afloat' |
   | 2. | nôu  | 'be awake'    | n̥ôu  | 'waken'      |
   | 3. | láʔ  | 'be bare'     | l̥áʔ  | 'uncover'    |

2. **Thematic roles:** Write three sentences of your own, and label thematic roles for each NP. You should have at least one example of each of the following:

   agent
   theme
   source
   goal
   location
   instrument

   _____

   _____

   _____

   _____

   _____

   _____

3. **Pragmatics and sentence interpretation:** Look at each snippet of conversation, and answer the questions that follow.

   a. Prosecution lawyer to defense witness: *Have you stopped taking drugs? Just answer with a simple yes or no.*

      If the witness has never taken drugs, can she answer the question? Why or why not?

   b. Doctor to patient with bursitis: *Can you reach the top shelf?*
      Short student to tall student in the library: *Can you reach the top shelf?*

      Is the implicature the same for both questions? Why or why not?

   c. A letter of recommendation for a student applying to graduate school: *I am writing to recommend Joe Blow for graduate study. He was my advisee, and I have always found him unfailingly polite and punctual. Also, he dresses extremely well. Sincerely . . .*

      What maxims are being violated? What is the implicature of the letter?

 **RECAP**

Make sure you know how to do the following. (See also the Key Terms on pp. 278–279 of the main text.)

- define connotation, denotation, extension, and intension
- do componential analysis
- spot fuzzy concepts, grammaticalized concepts, and lexicalized concepts
- spot the semantic basis for different word classes
- identify the semantic relations between words
- identify the semantic relations between sentences
- spot lexical ambiguity
- spot and represent structural ambiguity
- identify noun phrases and their thematic roles
- identify the effect of world knowledge in sentence interpretation
- identify when presupposition occurs in sentence interpretation
- spot the different forms of deictic terms
- identify conversational principles and maxims

## QUESTIONS? PROBLEMS?

*seven*

# HISTORICAL LINGUISTICS: THE STUDY OF LANGUAGE CHANGE

Historical linguistics studies the principles governing language change. This branch of linguistics is concerned with both the description and explanation of language change. Following are some of the important topics and concepts covered in this chapter. Make sure you are familiar with them.

Causes of language change

Sound change

Phonological change

Morphological change

Syntactic change

Lexical change

Semantic change

Comparative reconstruction

Indo-European and the development of English

## CAUSES OF LANGUAGE CHANGE (Section 1.2, pp. 291–293)

It is a well-known fact that language is always changing. Language change is regular and systematic. Language changes because of the way language is acquired. Children are not born with a complete grammar, but must construct a grammar based on the language to which they are exposed. Therefore, changes will occur from one generation to the next, and because all children have the same genetic capabilities for language and construct their grammars in similar fashions, the same patterns of change are found within and across languages.

There are five basic causes of language change.

- Articulatory simplification

  These are sound changes that occur simply to make a word easier to pronounce.

  For example, it is easier to pronounce the word *fifths* without [θ], as in [fɪfs], than with the [θ], as in [fɪfθs].

- Spelling

  Spelling is always slow to change. Therefore, many spellings reflect older pronunciations. Sometimes pronunciations revert to an older form, which is still reflected in the spelling of the word.

For example, the word *often* was initially pronounced with a [t], as in [ɔftən]. Later, the [t] became silent, changing the word's pronunciation to [ɔfən]. However, the letter *t* was retained in the word's spelling, and this sound is now being introduced back into many speakers' pronunciation, making it once again [ɔftən].

- Analogy

  Languages tend to prefer regular patterns. Exceptions or irregular patterns, therefore, are occasionally regularized based on comparisons with the regular paradigms.

  For example, many verbs in English use vowel alternations to mark a change in tense (e.g., *swing/swung* and *sting/stung*). Based on similarities to this pattern, some speakers use *brung* instead of *brought* as the past tense of *bring*.

- Reanalysis

  Languages often borrow words from one another. However, the morphological structure of words can vary from language to language. Borrowed words are sometimes reanalyzed to fit the structure of the new language, thereby creating new morphemes.

  For example, the word *hamburger* originated as a German word containing two morphemes: the root *hamburg* and the affix *er*. However, in English this word has been reanalyzed into the morpheme *ham* and the (new) morpheme *burger,* which has since combined with other existing morphemes to create words such as *chicken burger* or *fish burger.*

- Language contact

  Languages do not exist in isolation. They come into contact with one another. And when this occurs, languages borrow from one another. Borrowing most often affects the lexicon of the language, but sounds can also be borrowed.

  For example, English has borrowed many words from Amerindian languages (e.g., toboggan, moccasin, tomahawk, Chinook). English has borrowed words from many other languages as well. Borrowed words are often called *loan words.*

## SEQUENTIAL SOUND CHANGE (Section 2.1, pp. 294–300)

While all aspects of a language's structure can change, sound change is often the most noticeable. There are many types of sound change that can occur, but most sound changes involve sequences of segments. The major types of sequential sound changes are outlined below.

- **Assimilation.** Assimilation involves sounds changing to become more like nearby sounds. Assimilation increases the efficiency of the articulations involved in producing the sequence of sounds. Such an increase in efficiency can result in articulatory simplification.

Some common examples include:

| Types of assimilation | Examples |
|---|---|
| a. Voicing assimilation<br>A sound becomes similar to a nearby sound in terms of voicing. | a. Early Old English [slæːpde] > Later Old English [slæːpte] |
| b. Place of articulation assimilation<br>A sound becomes similar to a nearby sound in terms of place of articulation. | b. Old Spanish [semda] > Modern Spanish [senda] |
| c. Manner of articulation assimilation<br>A consonant changes its manner of articulation to be like a nearby sound. | c. Early Old English [stefn] > Later Old English [stemn] |
| d. Total assimilation<br>A sound assimilates totally to a following sound. | d. Latin [septem] > Italian [sette] |
| e. Nasalization<br>A vowel becomes nasal near a nasal sound. | e. Latin [vinum] > Old French [vĩn] |
| f. Palatalization<br>A nonpalatal sound becomes or moves toward the palatal sound. This usually occurs near a sound that is made with the tongue at or near the hard palate—usually [j] or [i]. | f. Old English [kirike] > Middle English [tʃirtʃe] |

The above assimilatory processes most often affect adjacent segments; however, assimilation can apply at a distance. *Umlaut,* which is responsible for irregular plurals such as *goose/geese,* is an example of such a process.

• **Weakening.** Full vowels have a tendency to reduce, or weaken, to a schwa-like vowel before they delete. Consonants can be defined along a strength hierarchy, shown below.

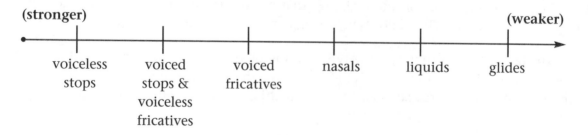

(stronger) ..... (weaker)

voiceless stops — voiced stops & voiceless fricatives — voiced fricatives — nasals — liquids — glides

Geminate (long) consonants are stronger than their nongeminate counterparts. The tendency over time is for consonants to weaken along a path determined by this hierarchy.

Some common examples include:

| **Types of weakening** | **Examples** |
|---|---|
| **Vowel weakening** | |
| a. Vowel reduction<br>   An unstressed vowel reduces to<br>   schwa. | a. Old English [naːma] ><br>   Middle English [naːmə] |
| **Consonantal weakening** | |
| a. Degemination<br>   A long sound becomes short.<br>   This is usually the first step in the<br>   weakening of consonants. | a. Latin [mittere] ><br>   Spanish [meter] |
| b. Frication<br>   A stop weakens to a fricative. This<br>   often occurs between vowels. | b. Old Spanish [maduro] ><br>   Spanish [maðuro] |
| c. Voicing<br>   Voiceless stops or fricatives weaken to<br>   voiced stops or fricatives. | c. Latin [maturus] ><br>   Old Spanish [maduro] |
| d. Rhotacism<br>   A fairly common type of weakening in<br>   which [z] weakens to [r]. | d. Gothic 'mai [z] a' ><br>   English 'mo [r] e' |

Consonants can also strengthen. Glides often strengthen to an affricate. This process is called *glide strengthening* and is common in word-initial position.

- **Deletion.** Deletion is often the end result of the weakening processes outlined previously. Both vowels and consonants may delete. Vowels are often subject to deletion when they occur in unstressed syllables.

Some common examples include:

| **Types of deletion** | **Examples** |
|---|---|
| **Vowel deletion** | |
| a. Apocope<br>   The deletion of a word-final vowel. | a. Middle English [naːmə] ><br>   Modern English [nejm] |
| b. Syncope<br>   The deletion of a word-internal vowel | b. Proto-Romance [vivər] ><br>   French [vivr] |
| **Consonant deletion** | |
| a. Consonants often delete when they occur<br>   as part of a consonant cluster, as the<br>   final consonant in a word, or as the last<br>   step after several weakening processes. | a. Old English [kneː] ><br>   Modern English [ni] |

- **Others.** There are other types of sound changes as well, many of which will be familiar to you from the phonology chapter. These types of sound changes are not as frequent as those already presented, but like assimilation, they also tend to have the overall effect of making sequences of sounds easier to articulate. Also like assimilation, these processes can affect adjacent segments or segments at a distance.

Some common examples include:

| **Types of sound change** | **Examples** |
|---|---|
| a. Dissimilation<br>   A sound becomes less like a nearby sound. | a. Latin [arbo<u>r</u>] ><br>   Spanish [arbo<u>l</u>] |
| b. Epenthesis<br>   A sound is inserted. This sometimes occurs to break up a consonant cluster that is hard to pronounce. | b. Old English [bræ<u>m</u>əl] ><br>   Modern English [bræm<u>b</u>əl] |
| c. Metathesis<br>   The position of two sounds has changed relative to each other. | c. Latin 'mira [<u>k</u>] u [<u>l</u>] um' ><br>   Spanish 'mi [<u>l</u>] a [<u>g</u>] ro' |

## OTHER TYPES OF SOUND CHANGE (Sections 2.2–2.3, pp. 301–302)

The changes considered so far have all involved segments changing under the influence of nearby, though not necessarily adjacent, segments. However, this is not true of all sound change that occurs in language. There are two other common types of sound change: segmental and auditory.

- **Segmental change.** Segmental change involves a change within a segment itself. Segmental change often involves affricates. Affricates are considered a complex segment, since they consist of a stop and a fricative.

Two common examples are given below:

| **Types of segmental change** | **Examples** |
|---|---|
| a. Affrication<br>   Palatal sounds (in particular, palatalized stops) become affricates. | a. Latin [<u>k</u>]entum ><br>   Old French [<u>ts</u>]ent |
| b. Deaffrication<br>   An affricate becomes a fricative by eliminating the stop portion. | b. Old French [<u>ts</u>]ent ><br>   French [<u>s</u>]ent |

The assimilatory process of *palatalization* is often the first step in the creation of an affricate. It is also possible to treat *glide strengthening,* a process in which a glide becomes an affricate, as an example of affrication.

- **Auditorily based change.** In addition to the articulatory considerations typically involved in sound change, auditory factors can also have an influence.

One common example is given below.

| **Substitution** | **Example** |
|---|---|
| One segment is replaced with a similar-sounding segment. | Middle English lau [x] > English lau [f] |

## PRACTICE 7.1: Identifying types of sound change

Each of the following exemplifies one or more sound changes. The older form is on the left, and the newer, more recent form on the right. Identify the sound change that has taken place for each of the underlined sounds.

1.  Proto-Quecha  [cum<u>p</u>i]   >   Tena  [cum<u>b</u>i]

    _____

2.  Old English  [<u>h</u>laf]   >   Modern English  [<u>l</u>of]

    _____

3.  Latin  [mar<u>e</u>]   >   Portuguese  [mar]

    _____

4.  Proto-Slavic  [<u>k</u>emerai]   >   Russian  [<u>tʃ</u>emer]

    _____

5.  Proto-Tupi-Gurani  [puʔ<u>am</u>]   >   Gurani  [puʔ<u>ã</u>]

    _____

6.  Latin  [orn<u>a</u>mentum]   >   Old French  [orn<u>ə</u>ment]

    _____

7.  Old English  [<u>kn</u>otta]   >   Modern American English  [<u>n</u>ɑt]

    _____

8.  Proto-Germanic  [do:m<u>az</u>]   >   Old Icelandic  [do:m<u>r</u>]

    _____

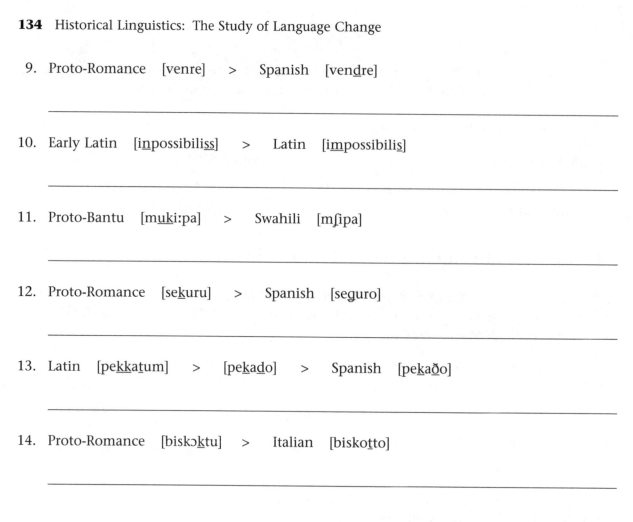

9. Proto-Romance [venre] > Spanish [ven<u>d</u>re]

_____

10. Early Latin [i<u>n</u>possibili<u>ss</u>] > Latin [i<u>m</u>possibili<u>s</u>]

_____

11. Proto-Bantu [m<u>uki</u>:pa] > Swahili [mʃipa]

_____

12. Proto-Romance [se<u>k</u>uru] > Spanish [se<u>g</u>uro]

_____

13. Latin [pe<u>kk</u>a<u>t</u>um] > [pe<u>k</u>a<u>d</u>o] > Spanish [pe<u>k</u>a<u>ð</u>o]

_____

14. Proto-Romance [biskɔ<u>k</u>tu] > Italian [bisko<u>tt</u>o]

_____

Sound change tends to occur in a step-by-step fashion, so a single sound can often be subject to a number of different sound changes. But these multiple sound changes are often not visible in the resulting form. Examine the following change that affected the word *good* in the development from Proto-Germanic to Old Icelandic.

Proto-Germanic [go:<u>das</u>] > Old Icelandic [go:<u>ðr</u>]

See if you can identify all the changes, including any intermediate but not visible changes that have affected the underlined sounds.

# PHONOLOGICAL CHANGE (Sections 2.4–2.5, pp. 302–305)

The sound changes described in the previous sections can influence a language's phonological inventory. That is, they can add, eliminate, or rearrange the phonemes within a language.

- **Phonological splits.** A phonological split adds phonemes to a language's phonological inventory. Allophones of the same phoneme become phonemic due to a loss of the conditioning environment. That is, sounds that were once predictable are no longer predictable and are, therefore, phonemic.

  Consider the following example in the development of English.

  Old English:     In Old English, /n/ had two allophones:
  - [ŋ] occurred before velar stops
  - [n] occurred elsewhere

  So a word like *sing* was pronounced as [sɪŋg]

  Middle English:   Consonant deletion applied to remove [g] at the end of a word (after a nasal consonant). This created a minimal pair between *sing* now pronounced as [sɪŋ] and *sin* pronounced as [sɪn]. And minimal pairs tell us that sounds contrast. [ŋ] and [n] are now separate phonemes.

  This split can be diagrammed as follows:

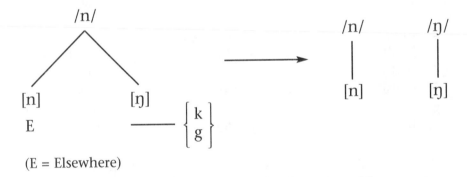

  (E = Elsewhere)

**Remember:** Spelling often lags behind sound change. We still spell *sing* with the final *g* even though it is now silent. Many silent letters in our English spelling system are a reflection of older pronunciations.

- **Phonological mergers.** While a phonological split adds phonemes to a language, a phonological merger reduces the number of contrasts.

  A good example of a phonological merger comes from Cockney English. In Cockney English, the interdental and labiodental fricatives have merged. That is, instances of [θ] and [ð] have become [f] and [v], respectively. In effect, [θ] and [ð] have been lost from the phonemic inventory.

- **Phonological shifts.** A phonological shift does not add to or diminish a language's phonemic inventory. Rather, some of the phonemes are reorganized with respect to each other.

The Great English Vowel Shift, beginning in Middle English, is a well-known example of this. The chart below gives the Middle English long vowels before the vowel shift occurred.

|  | FRONT | CENTRAL | BACK |
|---|---|---|---|
| HIGH | iː | | uː |
| MID | eː ɛː | | oː ɔː |
| LOW | | aː | |

## PRACTICE 7.2: The Great English Vowel Shift

Look at the words in Middle English and their pronunciation in Modern English. On the vowel chart below the list, draw arrows to show how the pronunciation of the vowel changed. Number each arrow to correspond to the number in the data set. The first one is done for you.

| | Middle English | Modern English | |
|---|---|---|---|
| 1. | [tiːd] | /tajd/ | 'tide' |
| 2. | [nuː] | /naw/ | 'now' |
| 3. | [seːd] | /sid/ | 'seed' |
| 4. | [sɛː] | /si/ | 'see' |
| 5. | [goːs] | /guːs/ | 'goose' |
| 6. | [gɔːst] | /gost/ | 'ghost' |
| 7. | [taːlə] | /tel/ | 'tale' |

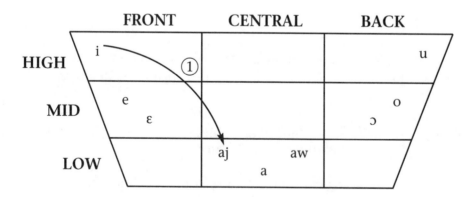

The Great English Vowel Shift probably began with the changes shown in *1* and *2* of the data set above. It then involved a shift up in vowel articulation of the remaining long vowels to produce the vowels that characterize Modern English.

Fill in the blanks to summarize the vowel shifts:

1.  Long [i] became the diphthong _____.

2.  Long [u] became the diphthong _____.

3.  Long [e] became _____.

4.  Long [ɛ] became _____.

5.  Long [o] became _____.

6.  Long [ɔ] became _____.

7.  Long [a] became _____.

As the vowels shifted, length was lost. After the Great English Vowel Shift, the long vowels now looked like:

|  | **FRONT** | **CENTRAL** | **BACK** |
|---|---|---|---|
| **HIGH** | i | | u |
| **MID** | e | | o |
| **LOW** | | aj    aw | |

As is evident by comparing the before and after charts, the overall effect of the vowel shift was a reduction in the number of vowels, thereby lessening the crowdedness of the phonological space. Note: Middle English also contained short (lax) vowels, which have not been included on the preceding charts.

**Remember:** Many of our vowel spellings reflect Middle English pronunciation. For example, *goose* is spelled with *oo* because this orthographic symbol represents [oː]. The word *goose* continues to be spelled this way, even though as a result of the Great English Vowel Shift, Middle English [oː] is now pronounced as [u]. One reason for this is that spelling was standardized before the vowels had finished shifting.

## MORPHOLOGICAL CHANGE (Section 3, pp. 306–311)

Morphological change affects the structure of words within a language. This type of change may increase or reduce a language's inventory of affixes. Recall from morphology that affixes are bound morphemes that attach to a base, and either provide grammatical information (inflection) or are used to create new words (derivation).

## Morphological Classification

Languages differ in how they combine morphemes into words. A distinction is often made between analytic and synthetic languages.

- **Analytic languages.**  These languages have very few inflectional affixes. Since English has only eight inflectional affixes, it is classified as analytic.

- **Synthetic languages.**  These languages have many inflectional affixes. Latin is a good example of a synthetic language.

The loss of affixes can result in a synthetic morphological system becoming analytic, while the addition of affixes can result in an analytic morphological system gradually becoming synthetic.

## Types of Morphological Change

Some of the common types of morphological change include:

- **Borrowing.**  New affixes can be added into a language through borrowing. Borrowed words frequently have a complex morphological structure. That is, they do not consist of a single morpheme, but have a root and at least one affix. Eventually, these affixes may enter the language. Two common examples are the suffixes –*ment* and –*able*. Words containing these affixes were initially borrowed into English from French as whole units. Later, however, these affixes came to be found on words that were not French in origin.

- **Grammaticization.**  Grammaticization creates new grammatical forms from lexical forms. Since grammaticization frequently results in affixes that are short, sometimes consisting of a single sound, lexical forms undergoing this process are often reduced phonologically. As well, much of the semantic content found in the lexical forms is lost. This is not surprising, as grammatical forms have less semantic content than do lexical forms. A good example of this is the development of the Italian future suffix -*ō* from the Latin word *habeō* 'have/hold/grasp'. As you can see, the original Latin word has been severely shortened and reduced in meaning.

- **Fusion.**  Fusion is a type of grammaticization. Like grammaticization, fusion involves the development of affixes from lexical forms. More specifically, it involves the development of an affix (either prefix or suffix) from two words that are frequently adjacent. Over time, these words fuse together to form a base and a suffix, or a prefix and a base (e.g., the Latin *amāre habeam* → *amābō*).

- **Loss.**  Affixes can also disappear from a language. Sometimes affixes just simply cease to be used. A good example of this is the derivational suffix -*bora* found in Old English, which attached to a noun (e.g., *mund* 'protection') to create a semantically different noun (*mund-bora* 'protector').

- **Reanalysis and analogy.** Recall that these are two of the causes of language change. Reanalysis can add new morphemes (e.g., *burger*) to a language. Analogy can change an existing morphological pattern (e.g., *brung* instead of *brought*).

## PRACTICE 7.3: Folk etymology

Folk etymology is used to refer to the analysis of a word that is based on an incorrect historical division of a word into its morphemes. This is usually done without reference to or study of the word's origins. Hence the use of the word *folk*.

Identify the base and affix for each of the following words.

1. yearling
2. duckling
3. gosling
4. underling
5. hireling
6. nursling

Are the words in the second column as common as those in the first? Does the affix have the same meaning?

Historically, each of the above words consists of a base plus the affix *-ing*. This German affix has the meaning 'having the quality of'.

a.  What happened to this affix in terms of its form? _____

b.  What happened to the affix in terms of meaning? _____

What might have caused this shift? _____

c.  What about the word *earthling?* How does this relate to the original affix as well as to

the above words? _____

What about the word *darling?* _____

## SYNTACTIC CHANGE (Section 4, pp. 311–314)

Change can also affect the syntactic component of a language's grammar. Change often affects the word-order patterns found in a language. It can also affect the transformations found within a language.

## Syntactic Classification

Languages are often classified according to whether they use case markings or word order to express relationships between elements of a sentence, such as the subject and direct object.

- **Case markings.** Case markings are inflectional endings found on elements such as the subject and direct object. These endings provide such information as to the agent (doer) of the action and the theme (entity undergoing the action). Recall from the semantics chapter that these are examples of thematic roles used in sentence interpretation. Languages with case markings often have a free word order. This is because the endings and not the order of the words provide the information necessary to interpret the sentence. Therefore, the order can be changed without disrupting the meaning. For example, the Old English sentence *Se cyning meteh thone biscop* means the same as *Thone biscop meteh se cyning*.

- **Word order.** Languages that do not use case markings must rely on word order to convey thematic roles. The three most common word-order patterns are SOV, SVO, and VSO, with the first two being used by the majority of the world's languages. Modern English is an SVO language, meaning that the subject is typically interpreted as having the agent role, and the direct object is typically interpreted as having the theme role. So, it is the position of these elements and not the endings found on them that is used for sentence interpretation, and changing the order of these elements will affect meaning. For example, the sentence *John hit the ball* and *The ball hit John* have different actors.

## Types of Syntactic Change

- **SOV to SVO.** Languages can change their basic word-order pattern. One common change involves the change from an SOV order to an SVO order. This is a change that happened in the development of English. English descended from a Germanic language having an SOV order.

- **Inversion.** Recall from the syntax chapter that Inversion creates *yes-no* questions from statements by moving an auxiliary verb in front of the subject-noun phrase. If the statement does not contain an auxiliary verb, then some form of *do* must be inserted. This was not always the case. In Old English, main verbs as well as auxiliary verbs could be inverted. Therefore, *Do* Insertion was not necessary.

## PRACTICE 7.4: Syntactic change in English

Below are some sentences from sixteenth-century English along with their modern counterparts. Examine the sentences, and determine how negatives were formed. How does this differ from today's English?

1. A kinder gentleman treads not the Earth.
   A kinder gentleman doesn't tread the Earth.

2. Hate counsels not in such a quantity.
   Hate doesn't counsel in such a quantity.

3. Clamber not you up to the casement then.
   Don't climb up to the casement then.

# CONNECTIONS

Changes can have far-reaching effects. A change that affects the phonology of a language can eventually affect the morphology, which in turn can affect the syntax.

Consider an example (somewhat simplified) of three stages in the development of English:

1.  Old English was a highly inflected language. Old English inflectional affixes included:

    - Case:        nominative, accusative, dative, genitive
    - Number:      singular, dual, plural
    - Person:      first, second, third
    - Gender:      masculine, feminine, neuter
    - Tense:       past, present

    Inflectional affixes were found on pronouns, nouns, articles, adjectives, verbs, etc. As in many inflected languages, Old English had a fairly free word order. Sentences with SVO, VSO, and SOV orders can all be found.

2.  During Middle English, sound changes started happening in unstressed syllables. These sound changes included:

    - m → n / _____#
    - n → ø / _____#
    - a, o, u, i, e → ə / _____#

    These three sound changes affected the inflectional system, since inflectional affixes in Old English were suffixes, and since suffixes are typically not stressed. The following examples illustrate the application of the above rules and their effect on the inflectional system.

    **OE**                                                    **ME**

    foxum  >  foxun  >  foxu  >  foxə
    helpan >  helpan >  helpa >  helpə

    As a result of these sound changes, all the affixes became the same: 'ə'. Since it was now impossible to tell what information was contained in an affix, the Old English affixes were dropped.

3.  But, speakers still needed to know what the subject of a sentence was, what the object of a sentence was, and what noun an adjective referred to. To get this information, speakers of English began to:

    - Rely on prepositions
    - Rely on fixed word order (SVO)

    So sound changes can have drastic effects on a language's development over time.

---

### REMINDER

Just as with phonological rules, sound changes often require an order to their application. For example, the three rules presented in the last section require some ordering. [m] has to first change to [n] before it can be deleted. If this change does not occur first, then [n] would not delete and the affixes would not all become [ə].

---

## LEXICAL CHANGE (Sections 5.1–5.2, pp. 315–319)

Lexical change involves modifications to the lexicon. There are two main types of lexical change: addition and loss.

### Addition of Lexical Items

New lexical items are typically added to a language's vocabulary in one of two ways.

- **Word formation.** Some of the word-formation processes found in the morphology chapter are frequently used to add new words to a language. These new words often fill a lexical gap resulting from technological innovations. Compounding and derivation are probably the two most frequently used word-formation processes for this purpose, although acronyms, backformation, blending, clipping, and conversion can also be used to add new words to a language.

- **Borrowing.** As languages come into contact with each other, they often borrow words from each other. There are three types of influences that languages can have on each other.

  - *Substratum influence.* This is the influence of a politically or culturally nondominant language on the dominant language in the area. Typically, the dominant language borrows place names as well as names for unfamiliar objects or items from the nondominant language. English borrowed place names such as Thames, London, and Dover from Celtic.

  - *Superstratum influence.* This is the influence of a politically or culturally dominant language on a nondominant language in the area. For example, English borrowed many words from the French language during the Middle English period. After the Norman Conquest, French became the dominant language, and many English speakers borrowed French words to increase their social standing. French loan words are typically found in relation to government (e.g., *government*), religion (e.g., *prayer*), judiciary (e.g., *judge*), science (e.g., *medicine*), culture (e.g., *sculpture*), and warfare (e.g., *army*).

  - *Adstratum influence.* This refers to a situation where two languages are in contact, but neither is politically or culturally dominant. Adstratum influence often results in the borrowing of common, everyday words. Such a relationship existed between English and Scandinavian speakers. Scandinavian loan words include *cake, egg, husband, score, window,* and *ugly.*

## Loss of Lexical Items

Words can also be lost from the vocabulary of a language. Loan words, nonloan words, compounds, and derived words can also be lost. The most common reason for the loss of a lexical item is some societal change that has rendered an object, and therefore its name, obsolete.

For example, English no longer uses the words *flȳtme* 'bloodletting instrument' and *eafor* 'tenant obligation to the king to convey goods,' the compounds *dimhus* 'prison' and *aelfscīene* 'beautiful as a fairy,' and the derived words *manscipe* 'humanity' and *heofonisc* 'heavenly'.

## PRACTICE 7.5: Lexical change

One of the reasons new and borrowed words are interesting is that they reflect a speech community's history—past conflicts, contacts, and advances. For this exercise, you will need to consult a good dictionary that gives etymologies for words. For each of the following words, find out from what language it is derived and when it entered the English language. Try to figure out why or how English added the word to the language.

| Word | Origin | When/Why/How Added |
|------|--------|--------------------|
| 1. plaid | _____ | _____ |
| 2. shepherd | _____ | _____ |
| 3. cherubim | _____ | _____ |
| 4. skin | _____ | _____ |
| 5. residence | _____ | _____ |
| 6. algebra | _____ | _____ |
| 7. portico | _____ | _____ |
| 8. theory | _____ | _____ |
| 9. moccasin | _____ | _____ |
| 10. jungle | _____ | _____ |
| 11. banana | _____ | _____ |
| 12. automobile | _____ | _____ |
| 13. boondocks | _____ | _____ |

## SEMANTIC CHANGE (Section 5.3, pp. 319–320)

In addition to the addition and loss of lexical items, the meanings of existing words can also change over time. There are seven main types of semantic change.

| TYPE | DEFINITION |
|---|---|
| Amelioration | The meaning of a word changes to become more positive or favorable. e.g., *pretty* 'tricky/sly/cunning' → 'attractive' |
| Broadening | The meaning of a word becomes more general or inclusive over time. e.g., *aunt* 'father's sister' → 'father's or mother's sister' |
| Metaphor | A word with a concrete meaning takes on a more abstract meaning without losing the original meaning. e.g., *high* → 'on drugs' |
| Narrowing | The meaning of a word becomes less general or inclusive over time. e.g., *meat* 'any type of food' → 'flesh of an animal' |
| Pejoration | The meaning of a word changes to become less positive or favorable. e.g., *silly* 'happy/prosperous' → 'foolish' |
| Shift | A word loses its former meaning and takes on a new but related meaning. e.g., *bead* 'prayer' → 'prayer bead' |
| Weakening | The meaning of a word weakens over time. e.g., *soon* 'immediately' → 'near future' |

## PRACTICE 7.6: Identifying semantic change

For each of the following words, identify which of the processes in the preceding table best captures the semantic change that has occurred.

| WORD | EARLIER MEANING | LATER MEANING | SEMANTIC CHANGE |
|---|---|---|---|
| 1. aisle | passage between pews of a church | passage between rows of seats | _____ |
| 2. mischievous | disastrous | playfully annoying | _____ |
| 3. blue | a color | being melancholy | _____ |
| 4. spill | shed blood | waste of liquid | _____ |
| 5. fond | foolish | affectionate | _____ |

6. butler    male servant in charge of the wine cellar    male servant in charge of a household    _____

7. passenger    traveler    one who travels by vehicle or vessel    _____

8. wretch    exile    unhappy person    _____

9. notorious    widely known    widely and unfavorably known    _____

10. chair    a seat    head of a university or college department    _____

# COMPARATIVE RECONSTRUCTION (Sections 7.1–7.2, pp. 324–330)

By comparing languages with each other, it can be determined whether they are genetically related. Genetically related languages are languages that have descended from a common ancestor. Using the comparative method, this ancestor can be reconstructed. This is typically done by comparing later forms to determine what the earlier form must have looked like. Although it is possible to reconstruct all aspects of a language's grammar, the focus here is on phonological reconstruction.

**Some important terms:**

• *Cognates* are phonetically and semantically similar words that have descended from a common source. Cognates are compared to reconstruct what this common source must have looked like.

• A *proto-language* is a language that has been reconstructed using a comparative method. Written evidence of what this language actually looked like typically doesn't exist.

• A proto-language consists of *proto-forms*. These are the individual reconstructed words of the proto-language. Proto-forms are usually indicated with an asterisk ( * ).

**Some important strategies:**

Processes underlying language change are systematic. Therefore, as you examine related languages, look for systematic phonetic correspondences that can be generalized for one language in relation to another.

• *The phonetic plausibility strategy* requires that any change posited to account for the differences between the proto-form (the ancestor) and the cognates must be phonetically plausible. That is, a sound change that has been found to occur in the course of language development must be able to account for these differences. For our purposes, the sound changes listed under the heading *sequential change* as well as under *segmental* and *auditorily based change* are all plausible.

- *The majority rules strategy* operates in the absence of a phonetically plausible sound change. This strategy states that when no phonetically plausible sound change can be determined, we may reconstruct the segment that occurs in the majority of the cognates.

## PRACTICE 7.7: Reconstructing phonemes

The following problems will give you practice in seeing systematic correspondences among phonemes of different languages and will guide you toward reconstruction of proto-forms.

1. **Proto-Algonquian: consonant clusters**

   Examine the following data and look for regular alternation patterns in the underlined consonant clusters. Note: None of the languages make a phonemic distinction between voiced and voiceless obstruents. In addition, in Menomini, [s] and [ʃ] are allophones of the same phoneme.

   First, sort the data so that you can see the four alternation patterns. Then, write the alternations in the list below the data set.

   | | Fox | Ojibwa | Menomini | Gloss |
   |---|---|---|---|---|
   | 1. | ki:ʃkahamwa | ki:ʃkaʔank | ke:skaham | 'he chops it through' |
   | 2. | netehkoma | nintikkom | netɛ:hkom | 'my louse' |
   | 3. | ahte:ki | atte:k | aʔtek | 'when it is there' |
   | 4. | nehto:wa | nitto:t | nɛʔtaw | 'he kills it' |
   | 5. | iʃihto:wa | iʃitto:t | ese:htaw | 'he makes it so' |
   | 6. | neʃki:ʃekwi | niʃki:nʃik | neske:hsek | 'my eye' |
   | 7. | ahkohkwa | akkikk | ahkɛ:hkok | 'kettle' |
   | 8. | mehtekwi | mittik | mɛʔtek | 'stick' |
   | 9. | aʃkotɛ:wi | iʃkote: | esko:tɛ:w | 'fire' |
   | 10. | no:hkomesa | no:kkomiss | no:hkomɛh | 'my grandmother' |
   | 11. | po:nihto:wa | po:nitto:t | po:nehtaw | 'he ceases from it' |
   | 12. | ----- | nantottank | nato:htam | 'he listens for it' |

   The four consonant cluster alternation patterns are:

   | Fox | Ojibwa | Menomini | Evidence |
   |---|---|---|---|
   | _____ | _____ | _____ | _____ |
   | _____ | _____ | _____ | _____ |
   | _____ | _____ | _____ | _____ |
   | _____ | _____ | _____ | _____ |

Now fill in the chart with the correct pattern beside the proto-form:

| *PA | Fox | Ojibwa | Menomini |
|-----|-----|--------|----------|
| *ʔt |     |        |          |
| *ʃk |     |        |          |
| *hk |     |        |          |
| *ht |     |        |          |

2. **Arabic:** [t], [d], [θ], [ð]

In the following data from Syrian and Iraqi colloquial Arabic, examine the alternations in [t], [d], [θ], and [ð]. First look for regular patterns; then determine what the proto-forms were. Fill in the chart to help you. Assume phonetic transcription.

[ɣ] represents a voiced velar fricative.

[ʕ] represents a voiced pharyngeal fricative.

[sˤ] represents a pharyngealized [s].

| | Syrian | Iraqi | Gloss |
|---|--------|-------|-------|
| 1. | daftar | daftar | 'notebook' |
| 2. | tneːn | θneːn | 'two' |
| 3. | ɣada | ɣada | 'lunch' |
| 4. | ʔaxad | ʔaxað | 'he took' |
| 5. | waʔət | wakɪt | 'time' |
| 6. | taːlɛt | θaːlɪθ | 'third' |
| 7. | dahab | ðahab | 'gold' |
| 8. | ʔaktar | ʔakθar | 'more' |
| 9. | maktab | maktab | 'office' |
| 10. | haːda | haːða | 'this' |
| 11. | tɪsʕa | tɪsʕa | 'nine' |
| 12. | duːd | duːd | 'worm' |
| 13. | sanduːʔ | sˤanduːg | 'box' |
| 14. | matal | maθal | 'example' |

a. Which of the four sounds does each language have in the following positions? Fill in the chart.

| Position | Syrian | Iraqi | Evidence |
|----------|--------|-------|----------|
| word-initial |  |  |  |
| word-final |  |  |  |
| between vowels |  |  |  |
| after a consonant |  |  |  |

b. How are Syrian and Iraqi different in the use of the four sounds?

c. What were the proto-forms?

d. What phonological changes have taken place to lead to the differences between Syrian and Iraqi? Remember: Phonological change can involve splits or mergers.

## Reconstructing words in a proto-language

We can move from a consideration of specific phonemes to more general reconstruction of words in the proto-language. We can see it best through an example.

**An example:**

Reconstruct the proto-forms for the data below.

| **Language A** | **Language B** | **Language C** |
|---|---|---|
| 1. hauda | hauta | hauta |
| 2. sav | ʃive | sav |

1. Determine the number of sounds that need to be reconstructed. This is straightforward for data set *1* in that all the cognates have the same number of sounds: five. The situation is different in *2*. In *2*, two of the cognates contain three sounds, and one contains four. If four sounds are reconstructed, then deletion must have occurred in languages A and C. If three sounds are reconstructed, then epenthesis must have occurred in language B. It is more plausible for deletion to occur at the end of words than epenthesis. Data set *2*, therefore, requires the reconstruction of four sounds.

2. Look for any total correspondences. These are sounds that have not changed; they are the same for all the cognates. Reconstruct these sounds. The proto-forms after this step are: *hau?a and *??v?.

3. Examine alternations between the different languages and determine phonetic plausibility.

   - Data set *1* exhibits an alternation between [t] and [d]. Either [t] or [d] can be reconstructed in the proto-form. If [d] is reconstructed, then the change from the proto-form to the form in language B ([d] > [t]) does not correspond to a sound change. Therefore, this has a low phonetic plausibility. If [t] is reconstructed, then the change from the proto-form to languages A and C ([t] > [d]) can be explained as an instance of weakening (a voiceless stop weakens to a voiced stop). This has a high phonetic plausibility. Reconstruct the change that has the highest phonetic plausibility. The proto-form becomes *hauta.

   - Data set *2* exhibits three alternations. First consider the alternation between [s] and [ʃ]. If [ʃ] is reconstructed, then the change [ʃ] > [s] in languages A and C has low phonetic plausibility since there is no motivation for it. If [s] is reconstructed, then the change [s] > [ʃ] in language B can be explained as palatalization. [s] is, therefore, reconstructed. Second, consider the presence or absence of a word-final vowel in the cognates. Recall from above that it is more plausible for a sound to delete than be epenthesized in this position. Therefore, [e] is reconstructed. Third, consider the vowel alternation between [a] and [i]. If [a] is reconstructed, then the change [a] > [i] occurs in language B, and if [i] is reconstructed, then the opposite change [i] > [a] occurs in languages A and C. Neither corresponds to a sound change, so both have a low phonetic plausibility. This strategy, therefore, cannot be used to reconstruct this segment. The proto-form, after this step, is *s?ve.

4. Any sounds for which no phonetically plausible sound change could be identified use the majority rules strategy. In data set *2*, the alternation between [a] and [i] cannot be accounted for using a sound change; therefore, [a] is reconstructed since it occurs in the majority of the cognates. The proto-form becomes *save. Notice that this proto-form does not correspond to any of the cognates. This is okay.

5. Put together a summary of the sound changes that have occurred since the different languages split from the proto-language. Remember that the form you have just reconstructed is older than the cognates from the descendent languages. Both voicing and apocope occurred in the development of language A, while only apocope occurred in the development of language C. Palatalization occurred in the development of language B.

---

## REMINDER

In order to do language reconstruction, you need to be able to identify phonetically plausible sound changes. And in order to do that, you need to know the different types of sequential, segmental, and auditory sound changes. Make sure you are very familiar with them.

## PRACTICE 7.8: Reconstructing words

To ease into reconstruction, try a couple of examples from hypothetical languages first. Then move on to real languages for the next exercises.

Each of the following data groups contains some cognate sets. Assume that all the cognates are in phonetic transcription and that all members of the cognate set have the same meaning. Reconstruct the proto-forms and list all the sound changes that have taken place in each language. Remember that for some languages, there may be no sound changes, while for others, there may be multiple sound changes.

While the data are from hypothetical or highly regularized data, it exemplifies processes found in actual languages.

1. **Hypothetical Language Group One**

| | Language A | Language B | | Proto-Form |
|---|---|---|---|---|
| 1. | mũtə | mudo | * | _____ |
| 2. | fumə | vumo | * | _____ |
| 3. | pippon | bipona | * | _____ |
| 4. | nõkə | noga | * | _____ |
| 5. | wusə | juza | * | _____ |
| 6. | fitə | vido | * | _____ |

Summary of Sound Changes:

| Lang A | |
|---|---|
| Lang B | |

**Remember:** The reconstructed form does not have to be the same as any of the forms found in one of the descendent languages.

2. **Hypothetical Language Group Two**

[x] represents a voiceless velar fricative.

| | Language A | Language B | Language C | Language D | Proto-Form |
|---|---|---|---|---|---|
| 1. | puxa | buga | puka | puk | * _____ |
| 2. | lizju | lizju | rizju | lizj | * _____ |

Summary of Sound Changes:

| Lang A | |
|---|---|
| Lang B | |
| Lang C | |
| Lang D | |

3. **Austronesian**

The Austronesian languages under investigation here are located in southeast Asia. Malay is spoken on the Malay peninsula and is closely related to Chamic languages. Chamic is a branch of the Austronesian language family brought to southeast Asia about two thousand years ago. Written Cham is the written form of Phan Rang Cham, a Chamic language of Vietnam. Tsat is a Chamic language spoken on the Chinese island of Hainan, off the south coast of China.

Your job is to reconstruct the Proto-Austronesian (*PAN) word for each of the words in the data set. Then below, summarize the sound changes.

| | Malay | Written Cham | Tsat | Gloss | *PAN |
|---|---|---|---|---|---|
| 1. | anak | anəʔ | naʔ | 'child' | _____ |
| 2. | sakit | hakiʔ | kiʔ | 'sick, painful' | _____ |
| 3. | ikat | ikaʔ | kaʔ | 'to tie' | _____ |
| 4. | urat | uraʔ | zaʔ | 'vein, tendon' | _____ |

Summary of sound changes:

| Malay: | |
|---|---|
| Written Cham: | |
| Tsat: | Tsat has also developed into a tone language (tones were not shown here). Why do you think Tsat has developed phonemic tones? |

4.  **German dialects**

The following data are from two dialects of German. Reconstruct the proto-forms for each word, and describe the changes that have occurred in the obstruents (stops and fricatives). You may not be able to reconstruct all the vowels accurately based on the amount of data here. Assume phonetic transcription.

[x]  represents a voiceless velar fricative.

[pf]  represents a voiceless labiodental affricate; it is a single segment.

[ts]  represents a voiceless alveolar affricate; it is a single segment.

| | Northern dialect | Southern dialect | Gloss | Proto-Form |
|---|---|---|---|---|
| 1. | maːkə | maxən | 'make' | _____ |
| 2. | ik | ix | 'I' | _____ |
| 3. | slaːpə | ʃlaːfən | 'sleep' | _____ |

4.  pʊnt          pfʊnt          'pound'        _____

5.  bejtə          bajsən         'bite'         _____

6.  dat            das            'that'         _____

7.  tuː            tsuː           'to'           _____

Summary of sound changes:

| Northern dialect: | |
| --- | --- |
| Southern dialect: | |

# INDO-EUROPEAN AND THE DEVELOPMENT OF
## ENGLISH (Sections 7.4–7.5 and Section 8, pp. 331–337)

The English we speak today differs significantly from the English spoken two hundred, five hundred, eight hundred, and even more than a thousand years ago. Using principles of language change and reconstruction, linguists can determine both what the ancestor of English was as well as what English must have looked like at some previous point in its history.

## Proto-Indo-European

In the late eighteenth century, Sir William Jones discovered that Sanskrit (the ancient language of India), Greek, Latin, and the Celtic and Germanic languages were all related. That is, words from these languages form cognate sets. It was eventually ascertained that at one time the people who now inhabit Europe and northern India all spoke the same language. Using the comparative method, linguists have been able to reconstruct the proto-language from which languages such as English, German, Spanish, Welsh, and Russian descended. This ancestral language is called Proto-Indo-European (PIE).

The speakers of Proto-Indo-European began a series of migrations from their homeland (possibly somewhere in central Europe). Within each migrating group, changes occurred to the proto-language until eventually each group spoke a different language.

In one group of speakers, the changes that occurred resulted in a language called Proto-Germanic. One of the main differences between Proto-Indo-European and Proto-Germanic was in the sounds of the two languages.

## Grimm's Law

In 1822, Jacob Grimm (of *Grimm's Fairy Tales*) noticed some regular sound correspondences between the Germanic languages and the non-Germanic Indo-European languages. These correspondences are listed below.

| Non-Germanic consonant | As in these non-Germanic words | Corresponding Germanic consonant | As in these Germanic cognates |
|---|---|---|---|
| [p] | pater (Latin) | [f] | father (German—Vater) |
| [t] | tonare (Latin) | [θ] | thunder |
| [k] | canis (Latin) | [h] | hound (German—Hund) |
| | | | |
| [b] | kannabis (Greek) | [p] | hemp |
| [d] | duo (Latin) | [t] | two |
| [g] | ager (Latin) | [k] | acre |
| | | | |
| [bh] | bhrata (Sanskrit) | [b] | brother (German—Bruder) |
| [dh] | vidhava (Sanskrit) | [d] | widow |
| [gh] | ghansas (Sanskrit) | [g] | goose (German—Gans) |

Grimm explained these correspondences using three sound changes. These sound changes are collectively known as Grimm's Law.

**(1) Voiceless stops became voiceless fricatives (i.e., weakening, specifically frication)**

| PIE | | PG |
|---|---|---|
| [p] | > | [f] |
| [t] | > | [θ] |
| [k] | > | [h] |

**(2) Voiced stops became voiceless stops**

| PIE | | PG |
|---|---|---|
| [b] | > | [p] |
| [d] | > | [t] |
| [g] | > | [k] |

**(3) Voiced aspirated stops became voiced unaspirated stops**

| PIE | | PG |
|-----|-----|-----|
| [bh] | > | [b] |
| [dh] | > | [d] |
| [gh] | > | [g] |

The above three rules capture the relationship between the cognates in terms of a sound shift. A sound shift is the systematic modification of a series of phonemes. The first of Grimm's rules involves the weakening of stops to fricatives. This, of course, is a phonetically plausible sound change. Sound changes that tend to occur across many languages are often referred to as natural. *Naturalness* is an important factor in reconstruction, since language change is regular and systematic. The result of this weakening process left Proto-Germanic without voiceless stops. Since it is rare for a language to completely lack voiceless stops, this gap was filled by devoicing the voiced stops. This change illustrates the role of *typological plausibility* in reconstruction: reconstruction should take into account the universal properties of language. The reintroduction of voiceless stops, in turn, created a lack of voiced stops. This new gap was filled by de-aspirating the voiced aspirated stops. This, of course, created yet another gap: a lack of voiced aspirated stops. This gap was not filled.

There are exceptions to Grimm's Law. Some systematic exceptions can be explained with a further rule, notably Verner's Law. Still other exceptions can be traced back to borrowings from Latin and French. Such borrowings did not undergo Grimm's Law or even Verner's Law, since these words entered the language long after the sound shift had occurred.

## The Development of English

Eventually, Proto-Germanic split into High German and Low German. High German developed into Modern German, while English began its existence as a dialect of Low German. Four Germanic tribes—the Angles, the Saxons, the Jutes, and the Friesians—brought Low German to Britain in approximately A.D. 450—the beginnings of Old English.

## PRACTICE 7.9: Grimm's Law

For each bolded sound in the reconstructed Proto-Indo-European (PIE) word, give the sound change that occurred as a result of Grimm's Law. Then give the Modern English equivalent of the proto-form.

| PIE WORD | GERMANIC SOUND (IN IPA) | ENGLISH WORD IN REGULAR SPELLING |
|----------|--------------------------|-----------------------------------|
| 1. *gel | _____ | _____ool |
| 2. *leb | _____ | li_____ |
| 3. *grebh | _____ | _____ra_____ |

4.  *ghreib          _____          _____ri_____

5.  *pulo           _____          _____oul

6.  *koimo          _____          _____ome

7.  *swad           _____          swee_____

# REVIEW EXERCISES

The items below provide a review of various topics covered in this chapter, particularly the history of the English language and comparative reconstruction on the basis of sound change.

1.  **The Great English Vowel Shift:**  For each of the Middle English words below, state the vowel change that would have occurred as a result of the Great English Vowel Shift, and then give the spelling of the corresponding Modern English word.

| Middle English | Vowel Change | Modern English Word |
| --- | --- | --- |
| a.  [noːn] | _____ | _____ |
| b.  [liːfə] | _____ | _____ |
| c.  [sweːt] | _____ | _____ |
| d.  [bɔːst] | _____ | _____ |
| e.  [guːn] | _____ | _____ |

2.  **Changes in English since Shakespeare:**  The quotations on the left are all from Shakespeare.  Some parts of the quotations are in boldface.  To the right are modern "translations" of the boldfaced elements.  Compare the early modern English of Shakespeare's time with contemporary English in:

   •  the word order of statements (think in terms of subject, verb, and object)
   •  the word order in negatives
   •  the word order in questions
   •  the use of pronouns and verbs that agree with them

Examine the data and answer the questions after the data.

   1.  From *Romeo and Juliet:*

Romeo: By a name
   **I know not how to tell thee** who I am.          I do not know how to tell you
   My name, dear saint, is hateful to myself

| Because it is an enemy **to thee.** | to you |
| **Had I it written,** I would tear the word. | If I had written it |

2. From *Hamlet:*

| Ghost: But, howsoever **thou pursuest** this act, | you pursue |
| **Taint not thy mind, nor let thy soul contrive** | Do not taint your mind or let your soul contrive |
| **Against thy mother aught.** | Anything against your mother. |

3. From *Macbeth:*

| Macb: I have done the deed. **Didst thou not hear** a noise? | Did you not hear/Didn't you hear |
| Lady: I heard the owl scream and the crickets cry. **Did not you speak?** | Did you not speak?/Didn't you speak? |

4. From *Macbeth:*

| Macb: **Saw you** the weird sisters? | Did you see |
| . . . **Came they not** by you? | Did they not come/Didn't they come |

a. What is the order of subject (S), verb (V), and object (O) in English today?

   What order of S, V, and O did Shakespeare use? Did he always use the same order? Cite evidence.

b. Where do we put the negator *not* in sentences today?

   Where did Shakespeare put *not*? Did he always put it in the same place? Cite evidence.

   What does Shakespeare's use of negation suggest about the time of the change in negation patterns?

c. What is the word order of *yes-no* questions in English today?

   What word order did Shakespeare use? Did he always use the same order? Cite evidence.

d. What pronouns did Shakespeare use that have fallen out of use today?

   What verb forms have fallen out of use along with these pronouns?

3.  **Sound changes in Romance:**  For the following languages, which have all descended from Latin, describe the changes that have taken place in consonants and in vowels on the edges of words. Given the small data set, you will not be able to account for every change, especially in internal vowels; however, you should be able to detail the process of change, including intermediate steps. Note: Latin is the proto-language here, so you are not expected to reconstruct it but merely to list changes that have occurred.

[ɥ]  represents a palatal glide articulated with rounded lips.
[β]  represents a voiced bilabial fricative.

| Latin | Italian | Spanish | French | Gloss |
|---|---|---|---|---|
| 1.  spina | [spina] | [espina] | [epin] | 'thorn' |
| 2.  scutella | [skodɛlla] | [eskuðija] | [ekɥɛl] | 'bowl' |
| 3.  scribere | [skrivere] | [eskriβir] | [ekriːr] | 'write' |
| 4.  schola | [skwɔla] | [eskuela] | [ekɔl] | 'school' |

Summary of changes from Latin to:

Italian:

Spanish:

French:

 **RECAP**

Make sure you know the following material. (See also the Key Terms on pp. 337–339 of the main text.)

- the five causes of language change
- the different types of sequential sound change
- the difference between sequential, segmental, and auditory sound changes
- the difference between synthetic and analytic languages
- the different types of morphological change
- the difference between case markings and word order
- the different types of syntactic change
- the different types of lexical and semantic change
- how change spreads through a language and its population
- how to reconstruct proto-forms and identify sound changes
- the three sound changes making up Grimm's Law
- the role of naturalness in language change
- the relationship between change and typology

# QUESTIONS? PROBLEMS?

_____

_____

_____

_____

_____

_____

_____

_____

_____

_____

_____

_____

# SOURCES

The following references provide background information for exercises that are new to the American edition of the *Study Guide*.

## Chapter 3

**Practice 3.4, #3, Japanese. Data derived from a number of sources:**

Fromkin, Victoria, and Robert Rodman. 1993. *An Introduction to Language. 5th ed.* New York: Harcourt Brace, 267.

Okada, Hideo. 1999. "Japanese." In *Handbook of the International Phonetic Association.* Cambridge: Cambridge University Press, 117–119.

Takahashi, Naoko. Personal communication.

**Practice 3.5, #2, Biblical Hebrew. Data from:**

Weingreen, J. 1959. *A Practical Grammar for Biblical Hebrew.* 2nd ed. Oxford: Clarendon.

**Practice 3.5, #3, German. Data from:**

Cowan, W., and J. Rakušan. 1998. *Source Book for Linguistics.* Amsterdam: John Benjamins, 7, 31.

Kohler, Klaus. 1999. "German." In *Handbook of the International Phonetic Association.* Cambridge: Cambridge University Press, 86–89.

Kurtz, John W., and Heinz Politzer. 1966. *German: A Comprehensive Course for College Students.* New York: W.W. Norton, 8.

**Practice 3.5, #4, Zinacantec Tzotzil. Data from:**

<www.zapata.org/Tzotzil/Audio/index.html>
<www.zapata.org/Tzotzil/Chapters/Chapt1.html>

**Practice 3.6, #5, Yakut. Adapted from:**

O'Grady, William, Michael Dobrovolsky, and Mark Aronoff. 1989. *Contemporary Linguistics.* 1st ed. New York: St. Martin's Press, 85.

**Practice 3.7, #1, Yuchi. Data from:**

Crawford, James M. 1973. "Yuchi Phonology." *International Journal of American Linguistics* 39, no. 3: 173–179.

**Practice 3.7, #2, Spanish. Data from:**

Dalbor, John B. 1969. *Spanish Pronunciation: Theory and Practice.* New York: Holt, Rinehart, and Winston, 59–65.

Gleason, H. A. 1961. *An Introduction to Descriptive Linguistics.* 2nd ed. New York: Holt, Rinehart, and Winston, 278.

Hadlich, Roger L., James S. Holton, and Matías Montes. 1968. *A Drillbook of Spanish Pronunciation.* New York: Harper and Row, 47–50.

**Practice 3.14, #1, Polish. Data from:**

Cohn, Abigail. 2001. "Phonology." In *The Handbook of Linguistics*. Edited by Mark Aronoff and Janie Rees-Miller. Oxford: Blackwell, 206–209.

**Review Exercise, #1, Passamaquoddy. Data from:**

Leavitt, Robert M., and David A. Francis. 1986. *Philip S. LeSourd's English and Passamaquoddy-Maliseet Dictionary*. Perry, ME: Passamaquoddy/Maliseet Bilingual Program.

Waponahki Museum and Resource Center. 1986–1987. *I Know How to Speak Indian*. Perry, ME: Passamaquoddy/Maliseet Bilingual Program.

**Review Exercise, #2, Kpelle. Data from:**

Welmers, Wm. E. 1973. *African Language Structures*. Berkeley: University of California Press, 30.

**Review Exercise, #3, Hausa. Data from:**

Schuh, Russell G., and Lawan D. Yalwa. 1999. "Hausa." In *Handbook of the International Phonetic Association*. Cambridge: Cambridge University Press, 90–95.
<www.humnet.ucla.edu/humnet/aflang/Hausa/Hausa_online_grammar/Grammar_frame.html>

**Review Exercise, #4, Bemba. Data from:**

Spitulnik, Debra, and Mubanga Kashoki. 1998. "Bemba: A Brief Linguistic Profile." Available at <www.emory.edu/COLLEGE/ANTHROPOLOGY/FACULTY/ANTDS/Bemba/profile.html>

**Review Exercise, #5, Syrian Arabic. Data from:**

Cowell, Mark W. 1964. *A Reference Grammar of Syrian Arabic*. Washington, DC: Georgetown University Press, 6–7.

Stowasser, Karl, and Moukhtar Ani. 1964. *A Dictionary of Syrian Arabic*. Washington, DC: Georgetown University Press.

**Review Exercise, #6, Malay. Data from various exercises in:**

Cowan, W., and J. Rakušan. 1998. *Source Book for Linguistics*. Amsterdam: John Benjamins, 30, 32, 190, 219.

# Chapter 4

**Practice 4.12, #1, Toba Batak. Data from:**

Crowhurst, Megan. 1998. "*Um* Infixation and Prefixation in Toba Batak." *Language* 74, no. 3: 595.

**Practice 4.12, #2, Turkish. Data from a variety of sources:**

Bender, Byron. Accessed through <http://www2.hawaii.edu/~bender/toc.html>.

Lewis, G. L. 1953. *Teach Yourself Turkish*. London: The English Universities Press.

**Practice 4.12, #3, Classical Nahuatl. Data from:**

Jordan, D. K. 1997. "Inadequate Nahuatl Reference Grammar" and "Nahuatl Lessons." Accessed through <http://weber.ucsd.edu/~dkjordan/nahuatl>.

Karttunen, Frances. 1983. *An Analytical Dictionary of Nahuatl*. Austin: University of Texas Press, xxvi–xxvii.

**Practice 4.13, #2, Turkish. Data from:**

O'Grady, William, Michael Dobrovolsky, and Mark Aronoff. 1997. *Contemporary Linguistics.* 3rd ed. New York: St. Martin's Press, 242–243.

**Practice 4.13, #3, Dutch. Data from:**

King, Peter, and Margaretha King. 1958. *Concise Dutch and English Dictionary.* London: Teach Yourself Books, Hodder and Stoughton.

<www.sr.net/srnet/InfoSurinam/dutch.html>

**Review Exercise, #1, Ancient Egyptian. Data from:**

Allen, James P. 2000. *Middle Egyptian: An Introduction to the Language and Culture of Hieroglyphs.* Cambridge: Cambridge University Press, 36–37.

**Review Exercise, #2, Luganda. Data from:**

<www.buganda.com/ggulama.htm#noun>

# Chapter 6

**Review Exercise, #1, Burmese. Data from:**

Ladefoged, Peter, and Ian Maddieson. 1996. *The Sounds of the World's Languages.* Cambridge, MA: Blackwell, 69.

# Chapter 7

**Practice 7.7, #1, Proto-Algonquian. Data from:**

Bloomfield, Leonard. 1946. "Algonquian." In *Linguistic Structures of Native America.* Edited by Harry Hoijer. New York: Viking Fund Publications in Anthropology, no. 6, 85–129.

**Practice 7.7, #2, Syrian and Iraqi Arabic. Data from:**

Clarity, Beverly E., Karl Stowasser, and Ronald Wolfe. 1964. *A Dictionary of Iraqi Arabic.* Washington, DC: Georgetown University Press.

Stowasser, Karl, and Moukhtar Ani. 1964. *A Dictionary of Syrian Arabic.* Washington, DC: Georgetown University Press.

**Practice 7.8, #3, Austronesian. Data from:**

Thurgood, Graham. 1996. "Language Contact and the Directionality of Internal Drift: The Development of Tones and Registers in Chamic." *Language* 72, no. 1: 21.

**Practice 7.8, #4, German dialects. Data from:**

Bloomfield, Leonard. 1984 [1933]. *Language.* Chicago: University of Chicago Press, 342.

**Review Exercise, #3, Romance. Data from:**

Bloomfield, Leonard. 1984 [1933]. *Language.* Chicago: University of Chicago Press, 335.

*Collins Concise Italian Dictionary.* 1985. Glasgow: William Collins.

Danford, Richard. Personal communication.

# ANSWER KEY

## CHAPTER 1

### Practice 1.1

1. Possible English words:  b, d, e, h
2. Possible English words:  b, d
3. Possible English sentences:  b, c, d, e

### Practice 1.2

1. All are examples of prescriptive grammar.
2. a. The first is prescriptive, the second descriptive.
   b. The first is prescriptive, the second descriptive.
   c. The first is descriptive, the second prescriptive.
   d. The first is prescriptive, the second descriptive.

### Review Exercise

a. 4 (answer supplied in text)
b. 1   c. 3   d. 2   e. 4   f. 4   g. 3   h. 2   i. 3   j. 4   k. 1

## CHAPTER 2

### Practice 2.1

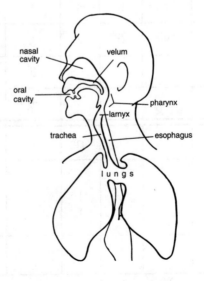

# Practice 2.2

1. consonant (answer supplied in text)
2. vowel
3. consonant
4. glide
5. consonant
6. glide
7. vowel
8. consonant

# Practice 2.3

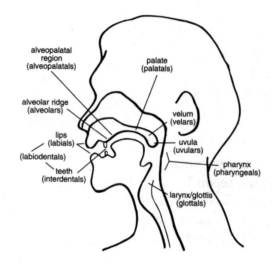

# Practice 2.4

| | | GLOTTAL STATE | PLACE OF ARTICULATION | | | | | | | |
|---|---|---|---|---|---|---|---|---|---|---|
| | | | Bilabial | Labiodental | Interdental | Alveolar | Alveopalatal | Palatal | Velar | Glottal |
| **M A N N E R   O F   A R T I C U L A T I O N** | Stop | voiceless | p | | | t | | | k | ʔ |
| | | voiced | b | | | d | | | g | |
| | Fricative | voiceless | | f | θ | s | ʃ | | | h |
| | | voiced | | v | ð | z | ʒ | | | |
| | Affricate | voiceless | | | | | tʃ | | | |
| | | voiced | | | | | dʒ | | | |
| | Nasal | voiced | m | | | n | | | ŋ | |
| | Liquid a. lateral | voiced | | | | l | | | | |
| | b. retroflex | voiced | | | | r | | | | |
| | Glide | voiced | w | | | | | j | w | |

## Practice 2.5

Words with aspirated voiceless stops:  2, 4, 6

## Practice 2.6

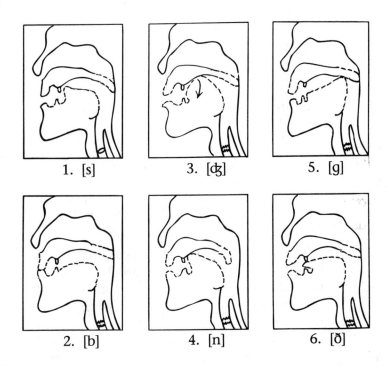

1. [s]     3. [ʤ]     5. [g]

2. [b]     4. [n]     6. [ð]

## Practice 2.7

1. [k]          3. [z]          5. [h]
2. [m]          4. [θ]          6. [d]

## Practice 2.8

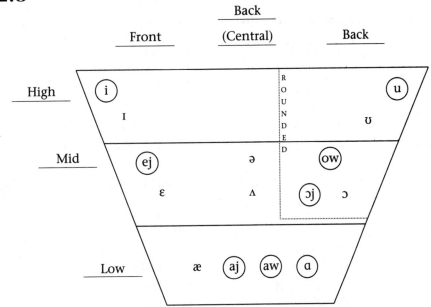

# Practice 2.9

1. Diphthongs are counted as single sounds.

    a. 3        d. 6
    b. 3        e. 3
    c. 5        f. 4

2. a. [t]       d. [n]
   b. [ʌ], [ə]   e. [ʧ]
   c. [k]       f. [i]

3. a. [f]       d. [m]
   b. [ŋ]       e. [z]
   c. [ow], [aw]  f. [s]

# Practice 2.10

1. [kræft]        8. [rɪʧ]        15. [θɔt], [θɑt]
2. [saj]          9. [tʰejp]      16. [hæd]
3. [hɛlθ]        10. [vejg]       17. [ɛgzɪt], [ɛksɪt]
4. [æʒɹ̩]         11. [rustɹ̩]      18. [ʃʊgɹ̩]
5. [frɔg], [frɑg] 12. [ɪnstɛd]     19. [junɪt]
6. [pʰædl̩]       13. [barm̩]       20. [kwɛsʧn̩]
7. [ejnʤl̩]       14. [ʧɹ̩ʧ]

# Practice 2.11

1. [kʰi]         5. [ʧiz]        9. [bown]
2. [du], [dju]   6. [ejt]       10. [ist]
3. [lowf]        7. [wiz], [ʍiz] 11. [bejbi]
4. [mejd]        8. [θru]       12. [θrow]

# Practice 2.12 (Note: Answers are subject to dialectal variation.)

1. [ʧɪr]         7. [ðɛr]       13. [ʧɛr]
2. [kʰɑr]        8. [star]      14. [skɔr]
3. [sɹ̩]          9. [hɹ̩]        15. [flɔr]
4. [ɔr]         10. [hɔrs]      16. [kʰɔrs]
5. [hart]       11. [hard]      17. [harm]
6. [ʃarp]       12. [ʃɹ̩t]       18. [θwɔrt]

# Practice 2.13 (Note: Numbers 4, 6, 13, 14, 17 will be different for raising dialects.)

1. [vɔjs]        7. [trajl̩]     13. [bajsɪkl̩]
2. [awɹ̩]         8. [ɔjli]      14. [prajs]
3. [ajz]         9. [prajz]     15. [ɛmbrɔjdɹ̩]
4. [sajt]       10. [saj]       16. [sajd]
5. [prawl]      11. [kʰawntɹ̩]   17. [ajs]
6. [najft]      12. [dawn]      18. [dejz]

## Practice 2.14

1. [slʌʤ]
2. [kwɑləɾi]
3. [lʌk]
4. [nejʃn̩]
5. [θʌndr̩]
6. [bəhejv]
7. [sɛpərejt], [sɛpərɪt]
8. [ənawns]
9. [hʌŋ]
10. [ʌvn̩]
11. [stʌf]
12. [ʌndr̩stænd]

## Practice 2.15

1. leisure
2. axe
3. worthy
4. once
5. shade
6. shy
7. sweet
8. tube
9. choice
10. mention
11. pipe
12. softened
13. phony
14. statue
15. square

## Practice 2.16

1. voiced stops (answer supplied in text)
2. voiced consonants
3. strident consonants
4. voiced sonorant consonants
5. back vowels
6. lax front vowels

## Practice 2.17

1. metathesis
2. assimilation (voicing, manner)
3. assimilation (manner)
4. assimilation (place, manner)
5. dissimilation

## Review Exercises

1. a. The lungs provide the air necessary for making speech sounds.
   b. The larynx is responsible for different glottal states such as voicing.
   c. The velum is one place of articulation in the oral cavity. Also, opening and closing the velum allows or prevents air from passing through the nasal cavity, creating nasal or oral sounds.

2. a. (bi)labial
   b. palatal
   c. uvular
   d. laryngeal

3. a. [ʔ]
   b. [i]
   c. [m]
   d. [θ]

4.  a. low front unrounded lax vowel
    b. voiced labiodental fricative
    c. (voiced) alveopalatal glide
    d. mid back (or central) unrounded lax vowel

5.  a. [u]          d. [ɑ]
    b. [aj]         e. [ɪ]
    c. [i]          f. [ʊ]

6.  Note: Primary stress is marked by the symbol [ˈ] before the stressed syllable.
    a. [ˈskɔrnd]                      f. [ˈdupləkət] or [ˈdupləkʰejt]
    b. [dɪsˈkʰʌvəri]                  g. [ˈdɪktejt]
    c. [ɛkˈsplowʒən]                  h. [ˈɑkjəpajd]
    d. [ˈʤinjəs]                      i. [ɪnˈfɔrməɾɪv]
    e. [mækəˈrowni]                   j. [ˈajdəlajz]

7.  Note: There may be dialectal variations. Vowels in unstressed syllables may also vary.

    1.  [dejz]                    11. [æʤɪtʰejt]              21. [nowm]
    2.  [zɪrɑks], [zirɑks]        12. [rowst]                 22. [sɪksθs]
    3.  [gɛs]                     13. [θʌm]                   23. [mæskjəlɪn]
    4.  [jɛlow]                   14. [bɑrgn̩]                 24. [prɛʃəs]
    5.  [sajn̩s]                  15. [məʃin]                 25. [fɔrmjələ]
    6.  [mowɾɾsajkl̩]             16. [sərawndəd]             26. [kʰamədi]
    7.  [ɛkstɪŋgwɪʃ]              17. [kʰastjum]              27. [græʤuejt], [græʤuɪt]
    8.  [ɪmpləmn̩t],              18. [rajɾɹ̩]                 28. [ɪrɪgejt]
        [ɪmpləmɛnt]
    9.  [ajsəlejt]               19. [tʰajmtʰejbl̩]           29. [ʌnfərgɪvəbl̩]
    10. [frajtn̩], [fraj?n̩]     20. [lɛmənejd]              30. [kʰɔld], [kʰald]

8.  a. m: fricatives;       ð: labials
    b. n: oral stops;       g: alveolar consonants;       t: voiced consonants
    c. ɪ: back vowels

9.  a. epenthesis
    b. deletion, nasalization
    c. epenthesis, voicing
    d. deletion, place assimilation, nasalization
    e. metathesis

# CHAPTER 3

## Practice 3.1

1.  no
2.  yes
3.  no
4.  yes

**Practice 3.2** (Sample answers are given; answers will vary.)

1.  (answer supplied in text)
2.  tuck: duck          wrote: rode
3.  cut: gut            buck: bug
4.  fine: vine          safe: save
5.  sip: zip            bus: buzz
6.  more: nor           sum: sun
7.  red: led            peer: peel
8.  tank: thank         bat: bath
9.  cheer: jeer         batch: badge
10. pine: fine          cup: cuff

## Practice 3.3

1.  [p]   occurs after [s] and between vowels when the first vowel is stressed.
    [pʰ]  occurs word-initially and between vowels when the second vowel is stressed.
    [p˺]  occurs word-finally and before a consonant.

2.  [l]   occurs word-initially, between a consonant and a vowel, and between vowels when the second vowel is stressed.
    [ɫ]   occurs word-finally after a vowel, before a consonant, and between vowels when the first vowel is stressed.
    [l̩]   occurs word-finally after a consonant.

## Practice 3.4

1.  Oneida:   [s] occurs elsewhere.
              [z] occurs between vowels (V____V).
    Since they do not occur in the same environment, they are in complementary distribution.

2.  Oneida:   [s] occurs elsewhere.
              [ʃ] occurs before [j].
    Since they do not occur in the same environment, they are in complementary distribution.

3.  Japanese: [ts] occurs before [u].
              [tʃ] occurs before [i].
              [t] occurs elsewhere.
    Since they do not occur in the same environment, they are in complementary distribution.

## Practice 3.5

1.  Arabic:   [h] and [ʔ] are separate phonemes.
              Minimal pairs:  1–5; 2–6; 3–7; 4–8

2.  Biblical Hebrew: [ð] occurs after a vowel; [d] occurs elsewhere.
              They are in complementary distribution and are allophones of the same phoneme.

3.  German:   [X] occurs after a back vowel; [ç] occurs elsewhere.
    They are in complementary distribution and are allophones of the same phoneme.

4.  Zinacantec Tzotzil:
    [p'] and [p] are separate phonemes.
        Minimal pair:  5–12
        Near-minimal pairs:  1-7; 4–10
    [k'] and [k] are separate phonemes.
        Minimal pair:  3–6
        Near-minimal pair:  9–11

# Practice 3.6

1.  English:
    Note: We assume diphthongs are single sounds.

    Corresponding short and long vowels are allophones of the same phoneme. They are in complementary distribution. Long vowels occur before word-final voiced obstruents; short vowels occur elsewhere.

    Sample representation:

    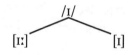

2.  Korean:

    Flapped [ɾ] and [l] are allophones of the same phoneme.

    Flapped [ɾ] occurs intervocalically; [l] occurs elsewhere.

    Representation:

    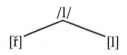

3.  Inuktitut:

    [u] and [a] are separate phonemes.

    Minimal pairs:  2–8; 6–10

    Representation:          /u/          /a/
                              |            |
                             [u]          [a]

4.  English:

    All are allophones of one phoneme.

    They are in complementary distribution: [gʷ] occurs before [u]; [gʲ] occurs before [i]; [g] occurs elsewhere.

    Representation:

    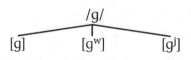

5. Yakut:

All are separate phonemes.

Minimal pairs:

[i] : [ɨ]   3–7
[i] : [y]   1–10
[i] : [u]   4–12
[ɨ] : [y]   5–9
[ɨ] : [u]   6–13
[y] : [u]   9–14

Representations:       /i/      /ɨ/      /y/      /u/
                        |        |        |        |
                       [i]      [ɨ]      [y]      [u]

# Practice 3.7

1. Yuchi:

   [t] and [tʰ] are separate phonemes.

   Both occur in similar environments, e.g., intervocalically, word-initially.

   Near-minimal pair:  1–11

2. Spanish:

   [b] and [β] are allophones of the same phoneme.

   [β] occurs intervocalically; [b] occurs elsewhere.

# Practice 3.8

Sample answers are provided:

### Practice 3.6:

   1. English
      2. /rɑbd/
      4. /mod/
   2. Korean
      3. /ilumi/
      4. /kili/
   4. English
      6. /rægu/
      12. /gis/

### Practice 3.7:

   2. Spanish
      2. /abana/
      3. /uba/

## Practice 3.9

Note: For the purpose of space, the word level is shown for the first answer only. However, the word level should be assumed for all subsequent words in the data set.

1.                                                      *open syllable

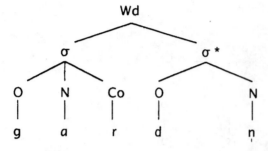

2.

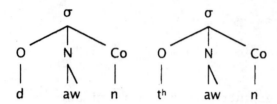

3.                                          *open syllable

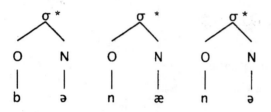

4.                                          *open syllable

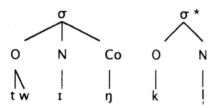

5.                                                      *open syllable

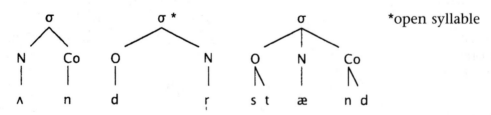

6.                              *open syllable

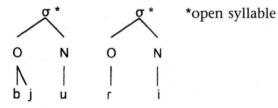

7.

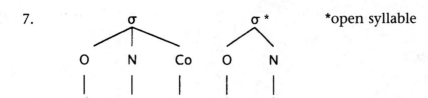

*open syllable

8.

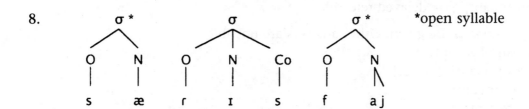

*open syllable

9.

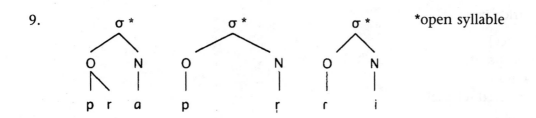

*open syllable

## Practice 3.10

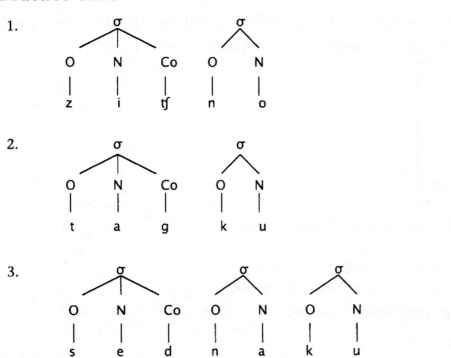

1.

2.

3.

## Practice 3.11

Stress in this language is on closed syllables.

# Practice 3.12

1.  a.  (answer supplied in text)
    b.  [+/– continuant]
    c.  [+/– strident]
    d.  [+/– nasal], [+/– sonorant]
    e.  [+/– continuant], [+/– delayed release]

2.  Note: Sample answers are given. Other answers are possible.
    a.  (answer supplied in text)
    b.  [ʃ]  [+continuant], [–voice]
    c.  [d]  [–continuant]
    d.  [w]  [+sonorant]

3.  a.  glides
    b.  voiced fricatives

4.  a.  [t]   [+voice]
    b.  [ʒ]   [+sonorant]
    c.  [m]  [–nasal]
    d.  [tʃ]  [–delayed release]

5.  a.  ODORSAL, [+high]
    b.  OCORONAL
    c.  [+sonorant]
    d.  [+voice] for both boxed groups; [b, d, g] are [–sonorant]; [m, n, ŋ ,l] are [+sonorant]

6.  a.  The sounds in the group share the following features:

$$\begin{bmatrix} \text{+consonantal} \\ \text{–sonorant} \\ \text{–syllabic} \\ \text{–nasal} \\ \text{+continuant} \\ \text{–lateral} \\ \text{–delayed release} \end{bmatrix}$$

The following features distinguish each sound:

| [f] | [v] | [θ] | [ð] |
|---|---|---|---|
| [–voice] | [+voice] | [–voice] | [+voice] |
| OLABIAL | OLABIAL | OCORONAL | OCORONAL |

   b.  The sounds share the following features:

$$\begin{bmatrix} \text{+consonantal} \\ \text{–sonorant} \\ \text{–syllabic} \\ \text{–nasal} \\ \text{–continuant} \\ \text{–lateral} \\ \text{+voice} \end{bmatrix}$$

The following features distinguish each sound:

| [g] | [ʤ] |
|---|---|
| [–delayed release] | [+delayed release] |
| ODORSAL | OCORONAL |

c.  The sounds share the following features:

$$
\begin{bmatrix}
\text{–consonantal} \\
\text{+sonorant} \\
\text{+syllabic} \\
\text{+continuant} \\
\text{+voice} \\
\text{OLABIAL} \\
\text{+round} \\
\text{ODORSAL} \\
\text{–low} \\
\text{+back} \\
\text{+tense} \\
\text{–reduced}
\end{bmatrix}
$$

The following features distinguish each sound:

| [u] | [o] |
|---|---|
| [+high] | [–high] |

d.  The sounds share the following features:

$$
\begin{bmatrix}
\text{–consonantal} \\
\text{+sonorant} \\
\text{+syllabic} \\
\text{+continuant} \\
\text{+voice} \\
\text{ODORSAL} \\
\text{–back} \\
\text{–reduced}
\end{bmatrix}
$$

The following features distinguish each sound:

| [i] | [ɪ] | [e] | [ɛ] | [æ] |
|---|---|---|---|---|
| +high | +high | –high | –high | –high |
| –low | –low | –low | –low | +low |
| +tense | –tense | +tense | –tense | –tense |

# Practice 3.13

## 1, 3. Rules and feature matrices:

Note: Full feature matrices are not given; only those features that distinguish the particular sounds are included in the feature matrices.

a.
$$\begin{bmatrix} \text{–sonorant} \\ \text{–continuant} \\ \text{+voice} \end{bmatrix} \longrightarrow [\text{–voice}] \quad / \quad \#\rule{1cm}{0.4pt}$$

b.
$$\begin{bmatrix} \text{+delayed release} \\ \text{0CORONAL} \\ \text{–anterior} \end{bmatrix} \longrightarrow \begin{bmatrix} \text{–delayed release} \\ \text{+continuant} \end{bmatrix} \quad / \quad V\rule{1cm}{0.4pt}V$$

c. $V \longrightarrow [\text{+nasal}] \quad / \quad \rule{1cm}{0.4pt}\underset{[\text{+nasal}]}{C}$

d. $[\text{ə}] \longrightarrow \varnothing \quad / \quad \rule{1cm}{0.4pt}\#$

e. $\varnothing \longrightarrow [\text{ə}] \quad / \quad [\text{p}]\rule{1cm}{0.4pt}[\text{l}]$

**2, 3.  Statements and feature matrices:**

Note: The rule using feature matrices follows each statement.

a.  A voiceless alveolar stop becomes glottalized following a glottal stop.

$$\begin{bmatrix} \text{–sonorant} \\ \text{–continuant} \\ \text{–voice} \\ \text{–SG} \\ \text{0CORONAL} \end{bmatrix} \longrightarrow [\text{+CG}] \quad / \quad \begin{bmatrix} \text{–sonorant} \\ \text{–continuant} \\ \text{+CG} \end{bmatrix} \rule{1cm}{0.4pt}$$

b.  Voiceless fricatives become voiced intervocalically.

$$\begin{bmatrix} \text{–sonorant} \\ \text{+continuant} \\ \text{–voice} \end{bmatrix} \longrightarrow [\text{+voice}] \quad / \quad \begin{bmatrix} \text{–consonant} \\ \text{+syllabic} \end{bmatrix} \rule{1cm}{0.4pt} \begin{bmatrix} \text{–consonant} \\ \text{+syllabic} \end{bmatrix}$$

c.  Nonlow tense front vowels become lax word-finally.

$$\begin{bmatrix} \text{–consonant} \\ \text{+syllabic} \\ \text{0DORSAL} \\ \text{–low} \\ \text{–back} \\ \text{+tense} \end{bmatrix} \longrightarrow [\text{–tense}] \quad / \quad \rule{1cm}{0.4pt}\#$$

d.  A voiceless oral stop becomes aspirated word-initially before a stressed vowel.

$$\begin{bmatrix} \text{–sonorant} \\ \text{–continuant} \\ \text{–voice} \\ \text{–CG} \\ \text{–SG} \end{bmatrix} \longrightarrow [\text{+SG}] \quad / \quad \#\rule{1cm}{0.4pt} \begin{bmatrix} \text{–consonant} \\ \text{+syllabic} \\ \text{+stress} \end{bmatrix}$$

# Practice 3.14

1. Polish:
Voiced stops are devoiced word–finally.

$$\begin{bmatrix} \text{–sonorant} \\ \text{–continuant} \\ \text{+voice} \end{bmatrix} \longrightarrow [\text{–voice}] \quad / \quad \underline{\quad}\#$$

2. South Midland and Southern American English:
[ɛ] becomes [ɪ] before a nasal consonant.

$$\begin{bmatrix} \text{–consonant} \\ \text{+syllabic} \\ \text{–high} \\ \text{–low} \\ \text{–back} \\ \text{–tense} \end{bmatrix} \longrightarrow [\text{+high}] \quad / \quad \underline{\quad} \quad \begin{bmatrix} \text{+consonant} \\ \text{+nasal} \end{bmatrix}$$

# Practice 3.15

1. Tamil:
Voiceless stops become voiced intervocalically.

$$\begin{bmatrix} \text{–sonorant} \\ \text{–continuant} \\ \text{–voice} \end{bmatrix} \longrightarrow [\text{+voice}] \quad / \quad V \underline{\quad} V$$

Derivation:

| UR | #kappal# | #mukil# | #kuṯi# |
|---|---|---|---|
| Voicing | —— | #mugil# | #kuḏi# |
| PR | #kappal# | #mugil# | #kuḏi# |

2. Gascon:
Voiced oral stops become fricatives between vowels.

$$\begin{bmatrix} \text{–sonorant} \\ \text{–continuant} \\ \text{+voice} \end{bmatrix} \longrightarrow [\text{+continuant}] \quad / \quad V\underline{\quad}V$$

A vowel becomes nasalized before a nasal consonant.

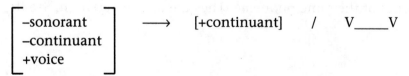

$$V \longrightarrow [\text{+nasal}] \quad / \quad \underline{\quad} \quad \begin{matrix} C \\ [\text{+nasal}] \end{matrix}$$

Derivation:

Note: Rules do not need to be ordered since they do not affect each other.

| UR | #taldepan# | #nobi# | #eʃado# | #umbro# |
|---|---|---|---|---|
| Frication | —— | #noβi# | #eʃaðo# | —— |
| Nasalization | #taldepãn# | —— | —— | #ũmbro# |
| PR | #taldepãn# | #noβi# | #eʃaðo# | #ũmbro# |

# Review Exercise

1. Passamaquoddy:

   [p] and [b] are in complementary distribution.

   [b] occurs between vowels; [p] occurs elsewhere. (Actually, the situation is a bit more complex, but this statement fits the data given here.)

   [p]  ⟶  [b]  /  V____V

2. Kpelle:

   Nasalized and oral vowels are separate phonemes.

   Minimal pair: 4–8

3. Hausa:

   [r] and [ɾ] are separate phonemes.

   Near-minimal pairs: 2–8; 3–7

4. Bemba:

   [s] and [ʃ] are in complementary distribution.

   [ʃ] occurs before [i]; [s] occurs elsewhere. This is a case of palatalization.

   [s]  ⟶  [–anterior]  /  ____ [i]

5. Syrian Arabic:

   The plain and pharyngealized consonants are separate phonemes.

   Minimal pair: 4–9

   Near-minimal pairs: 2–14; 6–16

6. Malay:

   [t] and [tʲ] are separate phonemes.

   Minimal pair: 2–7

   [tʲ] and [tʃ] are allophones of the same phoneme. They are in free variation. See the pair 3–14.

# CHAPTER 4

## Practice 4.1

1. insert = 1
2. memory = 1

3. format = 1
4. flowchart = 2

5. bug = 1
6. debug = 2

7. supply = 1
8. supplies = 2
9. supplier = 2

10. faster = 2
11. power = 1
12. processor = 2

## Practice 4.2

| | # of Morphemes | Free | Bound |
|---|---|---|---|
| 1. | (answer supplied in text) | | |
| 2. | 1 | wicked | |
| 3. | 2 | valid | in- |
| 4. | 1 | invalid | |
| 5. | 2 | Jack | -s |
| 6. | 4 | opt | -tion, -al, -ity |
| 7. | 2 | furnish | re- |
| 8. | 4 | able | in-, -ity, -s |
| 9. | 4 | nation | de-, al-, -ize |
| 10. | 1 | present | |
| 11. | 4 | act | -ive, -ate, -tion |

## Practice 4.3

| | # of Morphemes | Root | Root Category | Word Category |
|---|---|---|---|---|
| 1. | (answer supplied in text) | | | |
| 2. | 2 | amaze | verb | noun |
| 3. | 3 | use | verb | adjective |
| 4. | 2 | honest | adjective | adjective |
| 5. | 1 | Baltimore | noun | noun |
| 6. | 3 | love | noun | adjective |
| 7. | 3 | history | noun | adjective |
| 8. | 3 | control | verb | adjective |
| 9. | 3 | person | noun | adjective |
| 10. | 2 | tree | noun | noun |
| 11. | 2 | fast | adjective | adjective |
| 12. | 3 | read | verb | verb |
| 13. | 2 | beauty | noun | adjective |
| 14. | 1 | child | noun | noun |

## Practice 4.4

1.

2.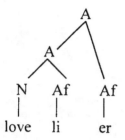

3.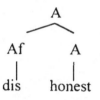

4.

5.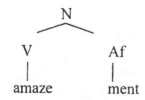

6.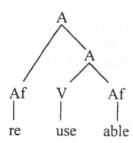

7.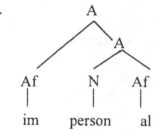

8.

    N
    |
    Baltimore

## Practice 4.5

| | **Lexical Category** | **Inflectional Information** |
|---|---|---|
| 1. | (answer supplied in text) | |
| 2. | V | third-person singular nonpast |
| 3. | A | superlative |
| 4. | N | plural |
| 5. | V | progressive |
| 6. | V | past participle |
| 7. | A | comparative |
| 8. | N | plural |

# Practice 4.6

| WORD | SIMPLE/COMPLEX | INFL/DERIV |
|---|---|---|
| 1. (answer supplied in text) | | |
| 2. fly | simple | —— |
| 3. prettier | complex | inflection |
| 4. stringy | complex | derivation |
| 5. delight | simple | —— |
| 6. reuse | complex | derivation |
| 7. triumphed | complex | inflection |
| 8. fastest | complex | inflection |
| 9. mistreat | complex | derivation |

# Practice 4.7

(Note: The affix is supplied.)

1. (answer supplied in text)

2. -y S
      N
  -y D
  -y S

3.    N
  -en S
  -en D
  -en S

4. -er S
  -er D
      N
  -or S

5. -er S
  -er D
  -er S
      N

6. -ly D
  -ly S
  -ly S
      N

7.    N
  in- D
  in- S
  in- S

8. -ed D
  -ed S
  -ed S
      N

# Practice 4.8

(Note: Sample examples are given in the tree diagrams; answers will vary.)

| COMPOUND | LEXICAL CATEGORIES | | |
|---|---|---|---|
| 1. bathroom (answer supplied in text) | | | |
| 2. scarecrow | V | + | N |
| 3. skin-deep | N | + | A |
| 4. bittersweet | A | + | A |
| 5. upstairs | P | + | N |

1.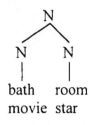
bath  room
movie  star

4.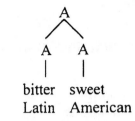
bitter  sweet
Latin  American

2.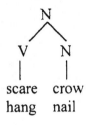
scare  crow
hang  nail

5.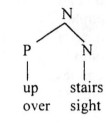
up  stairs
over  sight

3.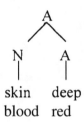
skin  deep
blood  red

## Practice 4.9

1. inflection

take  en

4. derivation, inflection
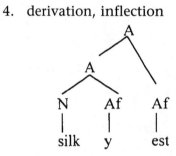
silk  y  est

2. compound inflection
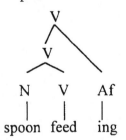
spoon  feed  ing

5. derivation, inflection
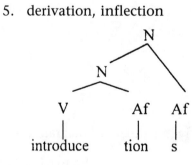
introduce  tion  s

3. inflection

soft  est

6. inflection

step  s

7. inflection

8. derivation, inflection

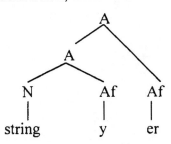

9. derivation, inflection

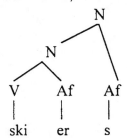

10. -----

11. compound

12. inflection

13. derivation

14. derivation

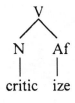

15. derivation

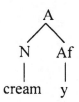

16. derivation, inflection

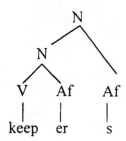

17. derivation

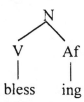

18. inflection

19. derivation, compound

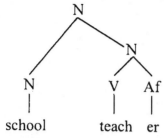

```
            N
          /   \
         N     N
         |    / \
      school  V  Af
              |   |
           teach  er
```

20. derivation

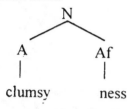

```
         N
       /   \
      A     Af
      |      |
   clumsy   ness
```

21. compound, inflection

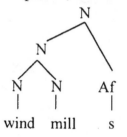

```
            N
          /   \
         N      \
        / \      \
       N   N     Af
       |   |      |
     wind mill    s
```

22. inflection

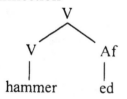

```
         V
       /   \
      V     Af
      |      |
   hammer   ed
```

23. derivation, inflection

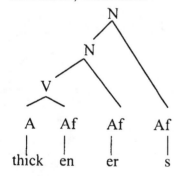

```
              N
            /   \
           N      \
          / \      \
         V   \      \
        / \   Af    Af
       A  Af  er     s
       |   |
     thick en
```

24. derivation, inflection

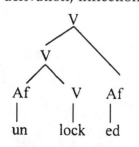

```
          V
        /   \
       V     Af
      / \     |
     Af  V    ed
     |   |
     un lock
```

25. derivation

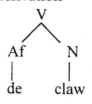

```
         V
       /   \
      Af    N
      |     |
      de   claw
```

26. derivation

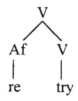

```
        V
      /   \
     Af    V
     |     |
     re   try
```

27. compound

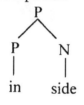

```
        P
      /   \
     P     N
     |     |
     in   side
```

28. derivation

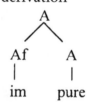

```
         A
       /   \
      Af    A
      |     |
      im   pure
```

29. compound, derivation

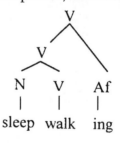

```
             V
           /   \
          V      \
        / | \     \
       N  V  Af
       |  |   |
     sleep walk ing
```

30. derivation, inflection

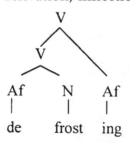

```
           V
         /   \
        V      \
      / | \     \
     Af  N  Af
     |   |   |
     de frost ing
```

## Practice 4.10

1. (answer supplied in text)
2. conversion
3. inflection (internal change)
4. compounding
5. onomatopoeia
6. inflection (internal change)
7. derivation
8. clipping
9. inflection (suppletion)
10. inflection (internal change)
11. cliticization
12. compounding
13. conversion
14. onomatopoeia
15. acronym

Words from the passage:

| | |
|---|---|
| enthuse | backformation |
| UCLA | acronym |
| profs | clipping |
| spoonfeed | compounding |
| smog | blending |
| sandwiches | coinage (from the Earl of Sandwich) |
| laze | backformation |
| scuba | acronym |
| dacron | coinage |
| dry suit | compounding |
| headache | compounding |
| sunstroke | compounding |
| flu | clipping |
| doc | clipping |
| lab | clipping |
| urinalysis | blending |
| blood test | compounding |
| ENT | acronym |
| OK | acronym (assuming the dubious etymology of 'oll korrect') |
| LA | acronym |
| ohms | coinage (from the physicist Georg Simon Ohm) |
| watts | coinage (from James Watt) |
| volts | coinage (from Count Volta) |
| MIT | acronym |

## Practice 4.11

1. Mende
   a. -i
   b. [salei]
   c. 'night'

2. Ganda
   a. omu-
   b. aba-
   c. [omulanga]

3. Kanuri
   a. prefix
   b. [nəm]
   c. [nəmkəji]
   d. [gəla]
   e. derivation
   f.
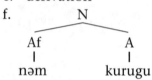

## Practice 4.12

1. Toba Batak
   a. -um- indicates comparative
   b. infix
   c. [dumatu] 'wiser'
   d. [sumɔmal] 'more usual'
   e. [ʤɛppɛk] 'short'
   f. [lógo] 'dry'

2. Turkish
   a. Morphemes

   | | | | | |
   |---|---|---|---|---|
   | 1. 'city' | [ʃehir] | 8. 'from' | -[den] |
   | 2. 'hand' | [el] | 9. 'to' | -[e] |
   | 3. 'bridge' | [kœpry] | 10. 'on, in' | -[de] |
   | 4. 'bell' | [zil] | 11. 'my' | -[im] |
   | 5. 'house' | [ev] | 12. 'your' | -[iniz] |
   | 6. 'voice' | [ses] | 13. PLURAL | -[ler] |
   | 7. 'bus' | [otobys] | | |

   b. Order of morphemes: ROOT + PLURAL + POSSESSIVE + POSTPOSITION
   c. English translation
      1. 'in a city'
      2. 'your hands'
   d. Turkish translation
      'to the buses' [otobyslere]

3. Classical Nahuatl
    a. Morphemes
        1. 'sing'                          [kʷiːka]
        2. 'eat'                           [kʷa]
        3. 'bathe'                         [aːltia]
        4. you (SG) (subject)              [ti]-
        5. s/he (subject)                  Ø (not marked)
        6. it (object)                     [ki]-
        7. we (subject)                    [ti]- (stem)-[ʔ]
        8. you (PL) (subject)              [an]- (stem)-[ʔ]
        9. they (subject)                  -[ʔ]

    b. suffix marking plural subject in present: -[ʔ]
    c. customary present marked with lengthening of final vowel plus suffix: -[ːni]

# Practice 4.13

1. English
    a. 3 allomorphs:  [ɪn], [ɪm], [ɪŋ]
        1. [ɪm] occurs before labials.
        2. [ɪŋ] occurs before velars.
        3. [ɪn] occurs elsewhere.
    b. [ɪn] is the elsewhere allomorph and is thus the underlying representation.
    c. UR of *inedible, impossible,* and *incapable* would all start with [ɪn].
    d. Place assimilation is at work.
    e. Rules:   [ɪn]   ⟶   [ɪm]   /   ____ C
                                          ₀LABIAL

            [ɪn]   ⟶   [ɪŋ]   /   ____ C
                                      ₀DORSAL

    The rules could also be formulated as one rule using alpha notation.

2. Turkish
    a. [lar], [ler]
    b. [+/–back]
    c. [+/–back]  If the last V in the root is [+back], the allomorph is [lar]. If the last V in the root is [–back], the allomorph is [ler].

3. Dutch
    a. -en
    b. ge-(STEM)-t/d
        -t is used when stem ends with a voiceless C.
        -d is used when stem ends with a voiced C or V.
    c. Both are pronounced as [t] because of word-final consonant devoicing.
    d. ge-
    e. *gestolen* is a strong verb. It has no -t/d suffix as would be expected with a weak verb.

## Review Exercises

1. Ancient Egyptian

   a. Morphemes:
      1. 'sibling'      sn
      2. 'deity'        ntʲr
      3. FEMININE     -t
      4. MASCULINE    Ø (not marked)
      5. DUAL         -j
      6. PLURAL       -w

   b. Order of morphemes:
      1. M SG:   ROOT
      2. F SG:   ROOT/FEMININE
      3. M PL:   ROOT/PLURAL
      4. F PL:   ROOT/PLURAL/FEMININE
      5. M DU:   ROOT/PLURAL/DUAL
      6. F DU:   ROOT/FEMININE/DUAL

2. Luganda

| SG | PL | STEMS | GLOSS |
|---|---|---|---|
| mu- | ba- | -ntu (1, 20) | 'person' |
|     |     | -wala (12, 18) | 'girl' |
| ka- | bu- | -ti (2, 16) | 'stick' |
|     |     | -tiko (9, 14) | 'mushroom' |
| ki- | bi- | -tabo (3, 4) | 'book' |
|     |     | -ntu (10, 17) | 'thing' |
| ku- | ma- | -gulu (5, 13) | 'leg' |
|     |     | -tu (8, 15) | 'ear' |
| mu- | mi- | -ti (7, 6) | 'leg' |
|     |     | -sege (11, 19) | 'wolf' |

3. Fore

   a. Morphemes:
      1. I          -[uw]        7. eat          -[na]
      2. he         -[iy]        8. yesterday    -[t]
      3. we         -[un]        9. today        -[gas]
      4. they       -[a:w]      10. will         -[k]
      5. we (DUAL)  -[us]       11. question     -[aw]
      6. they (DUAL) -[a:s]     12. statement    -[i]

   b. Order of morphemes:
      V; adverb (tense); personal pronoun; question/statement marker

   c. Translations:
      1. 'He ate yesterday?'      [natiyaw]
      2. 'They (DUAL) will eat?'  [naka:saw]
      3. 'They ate today.'        [nagasa:wi]

# CHAPTER 5

## Practice 5.1

1.  
V Conj Pron P  
beat and she to  

Det N V N N N V  
the door located hobo jungle bum heard

2.  
N V P  
leg said in

3.  
Conj Det A N V Pron Aux V P  
and the great explorer says it could be in

4.  
Pron V N N N V Aux A N  
I turned key lab door thought would dull day  

V C Pron Aux V V  
noticed that my had flopped waving  

Pron V  
I realized

5.  
V A N V Aux  
was green clarity diluted was  

V A N Pron V N  
making cutting remarks she drank scotch

6.  
V N Adv  
hate pineapples dolefully

7.  
Det N A N Pron Aux V N  
a fortune male deer you will have bucks

## Practice 5.2

|  | HEAD (Lexical category) | SPECIFIER | COMPLEMENT |
|---|---|---|---|
| 1. | (answer supplied in text) | | |
| 2. | men (N) | —— | —— |
| 3. | in (P) | —— | the barn |
| 4. | mean (A) | really | —— |
| 5. | worked (V) | —— | —— |
| 6. | worked (V) | —— | at the station |
| 7. | boring (A) | extremely | —— |
| 8. | destruction (N) | that | of the city |
| 9. | walks (V) | never | to the park |
| 10. | small (A) | very | —— |
| 11. | in (P) | —— | the room |
| 12. | cute (A) | awfully | —— |
| 13. | smiles (V) | seldom | —— |

| HEAD | SPECIFIER | COMPLEMENT |
|------|-----------|------------|
| 14. fond (A) | rather | of apples |
| 15. swept (V) | —— | the floor |
| 16. poem (N) | the | about love |
| 17. pancakes (N) | —— | —— |

## Practice 5.3

Note: Answers will vary. Sample answers are given here.

1. very happy
2. never eats breakfast
3. read the newspaper
4. teachers of English

5. the apple
6. put the car in the garage
7. fond of her
8. often arrives on time

## Practice 5.4

Note: Sample answers are given. Some answers may vary.

1. Substitution test:

    1. [They] arrived [there] [then].
    2. *The cabbage [them] salty.
       Not a phrase.
    3. They moved [it].
    4. Little Andrew swallowed [them].
    5. Brendan is [doing so].

2. Movement test:

    1. *[Army was surrounded] the by the enemy.
       Not a phrase.
    2. [Viennese waltzes and Argentinean tangos] Leona likes.
    3. [In the revolving restaurant], Jean ate his lunch.
    4. *[Be merry for] eat, drink, and today will become yesterday.
       Not a phrase.
    5. *[Were swimming across] the polar bears the lake.
       Not a phrase.

3. Coordination test:

| | Conjunction | Substitution | Type of phrase |
|---|-------------|--------------|----------------|
| 1. | [the new desk] and [the old chair] | they | NP |
| 2. | [assembled the new desk] and [painted the old chair] | did so | VP |
| 3. | [new] and [expensive] | (no pro-form) | AP |
| 4. | [in a hole] or [under a rock] | there | PP |
| 5. | [rather huge] but [somewhat ugly] | (no pro-form) | AP |
| 6. | [worked on a movie] and [played in a band] | did so | VP |
| 7. | [beside the fence] or [near the tree] | there | PP |

8. [really lovely] but            (no pro-form)      AP
   [hideously expensive]
9. [talked to the girls] and      did so             VP
   [played with the boys]
10. [a dentist] or [a lawyer]      she                NP

# Practice 5.5

1.

2.

3.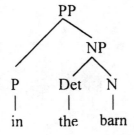

4.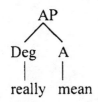

5.

6.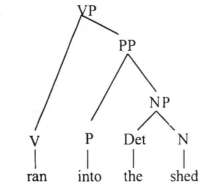

7.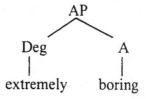

8.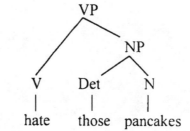

9.

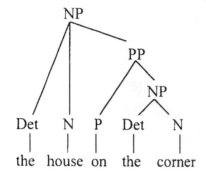

10.

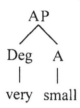

11.

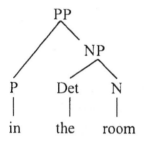

12.

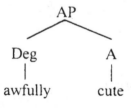

13.

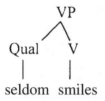

14.

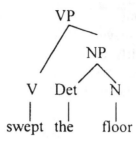

15.

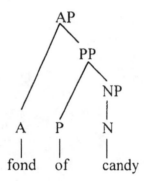

16.

17.

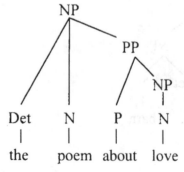

18.

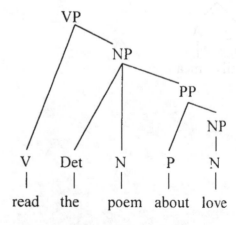

19.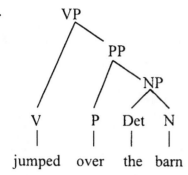

20.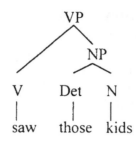

## Practice 5.6

1. Subcategorization options for verbs:
   (Note: Sample sentences are given, but answers will vary.)

   | Complement options | Sample sentences |
   |---|---|
   | 1. No complement: | When we saw the price of the dinner, we panicked. |
   | | *We panicked the price. |
   | 2. NP | We watched the show. |
   | 3. NP or | I can't imagine it. |
   |     CP | The child imagined that she was an astronaut. |
   | 4. NP or | Mark Twain wrote a book. |
   |     NP, PP or | He wrote a letter to his sister. |
   |     NP, NP | He wrote his sister a letter. |
   | 5. CP or | We wondered what was happening. |
   |     PP | They wondered about the story. |
   | 6. Ø or | The children played. |
   |     NP | The Cardinals play baseball. |

2. Subcategorization options for nouns, adjectives, prepositions:

   1. PP or CP        4. Ø
   2. NP              5. NP
   3. PP              6. PP or Ø

## Practice 5.7

1.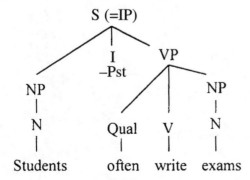

2.

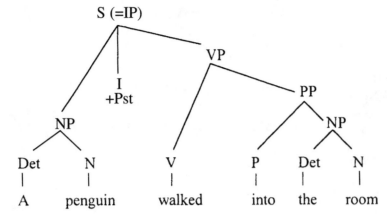

3.

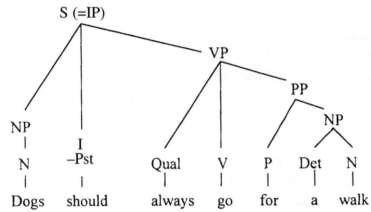

4.

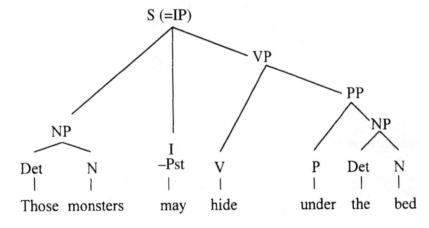

5.

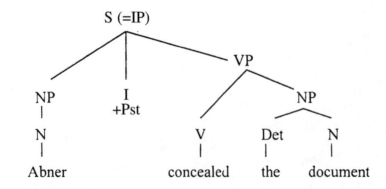

6.

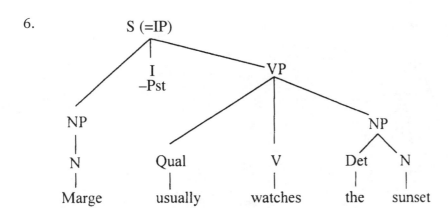

7.

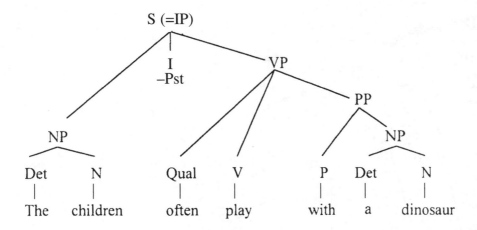

8.

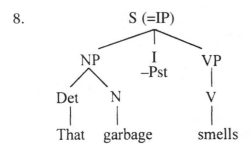

9.

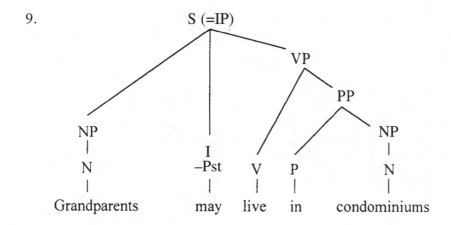

10.

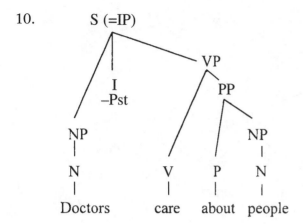

## Practice 5.8

1.

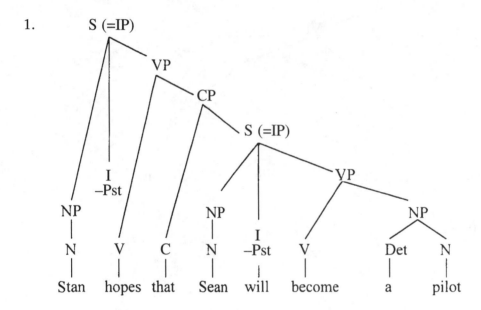

2.

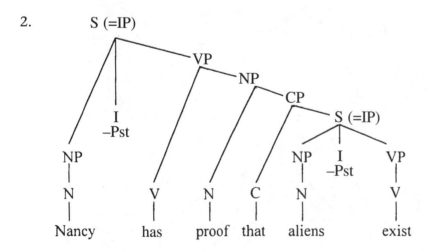

3.

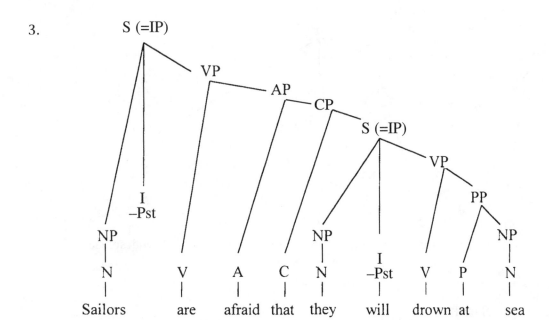

4.

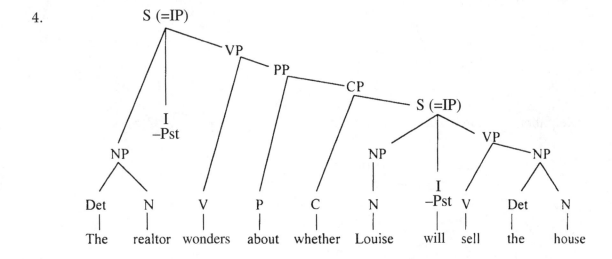

5.

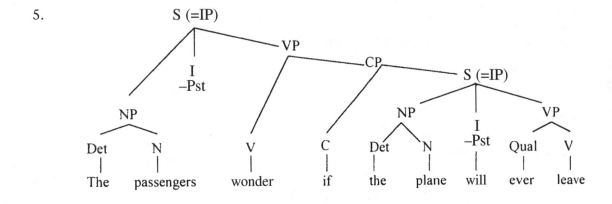

6.

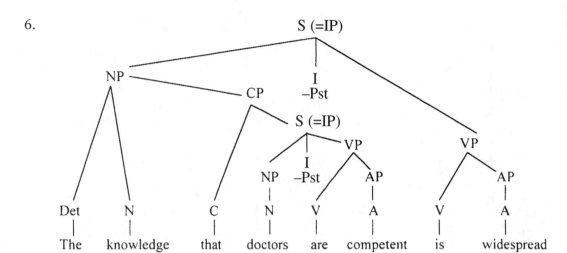

## Practice 5.9

1.

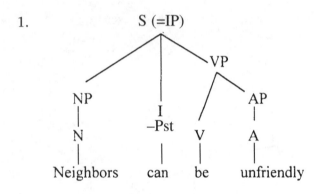

2.

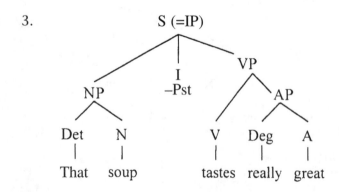

3.

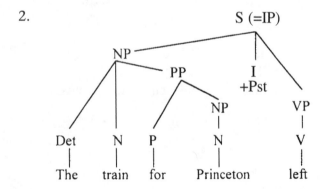

4.

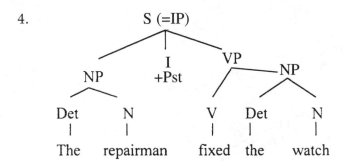

5.

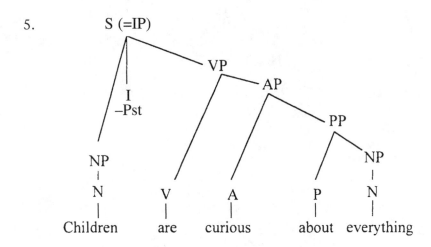

6.

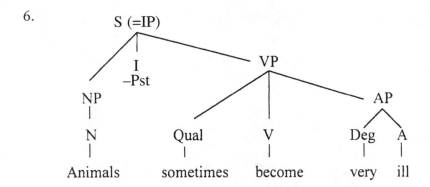

7.

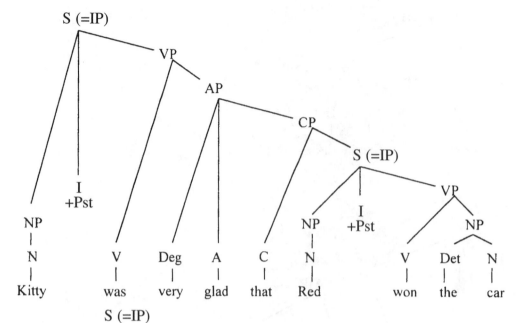

8.

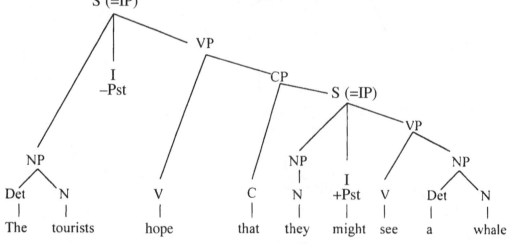

9.

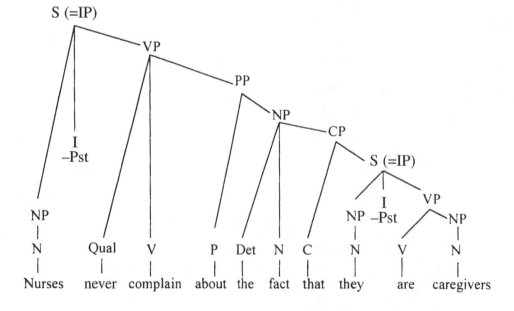

10.

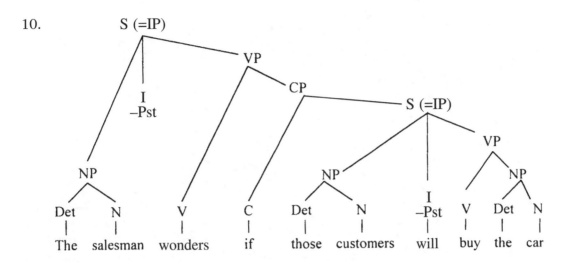

## Practice 5.10

1. Inversion
2. Inversion, *Wh* Movement
3. *Do* Insertion, Inversion
4. *Do* Insertion, Inversion, *Wh* Movement
5. Inversion

## Practice 5.11

(Note: The tree diagrams show the deep structure. Transformations are listed. At deep structure, the verb shows no tense or agreement since these features are contained in I.)

1. Inversion

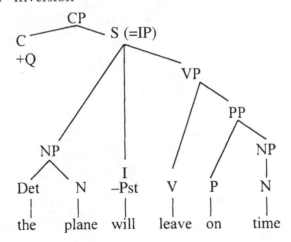

2. *Do* Insertion, Inversion, *Wh* Movement

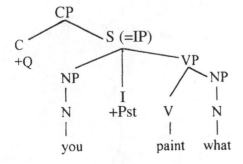

3. *Do* Insertion, Inversion

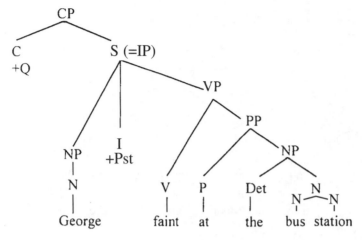

4. NP Movement

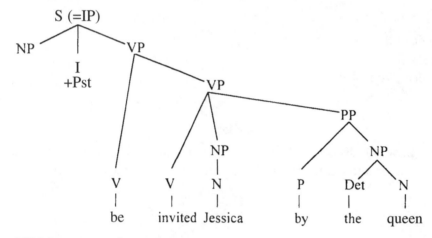

5. NP Movement, Inversion

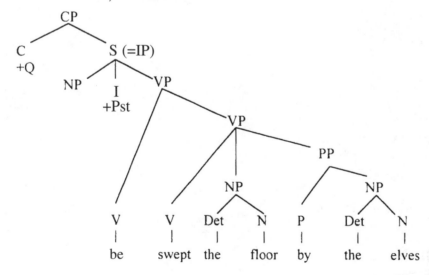

# Practice 5.12

1.  Inversion

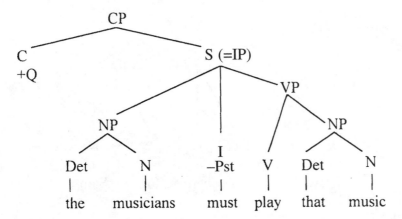

2.  *Do* Insertion, Inversion, *Wh* Movement

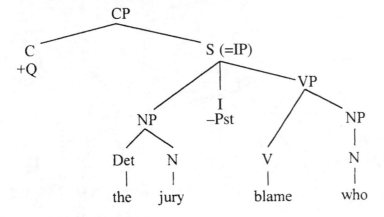

3.  (no transformations)

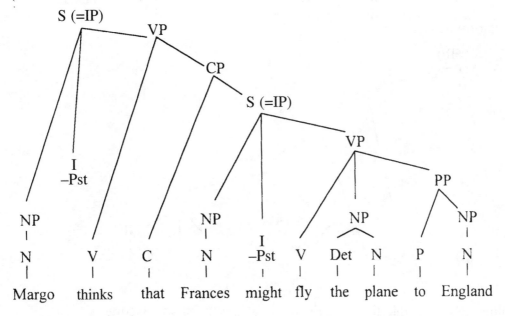

4. *Do* Insertion, Inversion

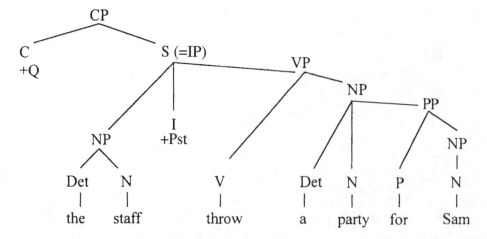

5. NP Movement, Inversion

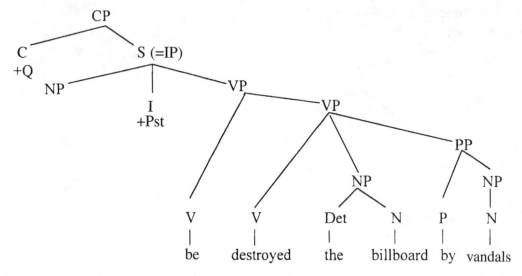

6. (no transformations)

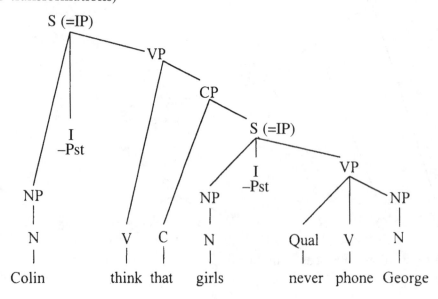

7. Inversion, *Wh* Movement

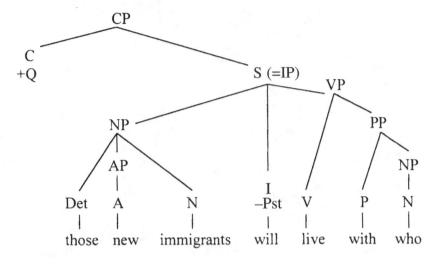

8. NP Movement

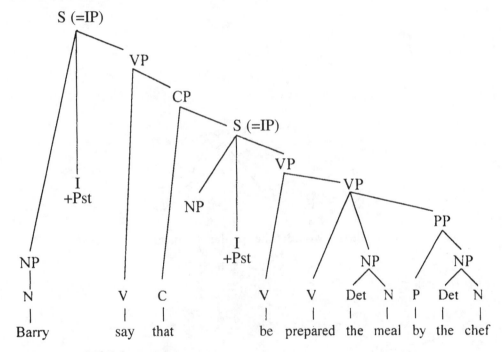

9. Inversion, *Wh* Movement

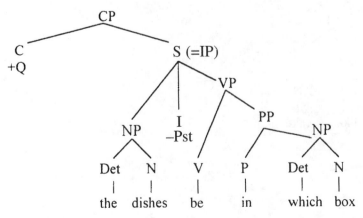

10. Inversion

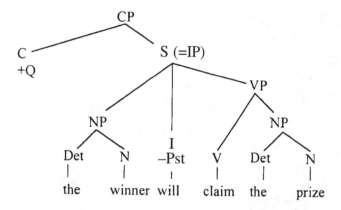

11. (no transformations)

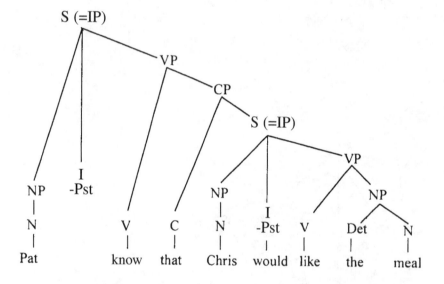

12. *Do* Insertion, Inversion

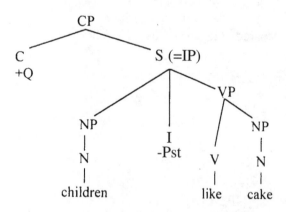

# Practice 5.13

1. Hypothetical language:
   a. shows that there is no inversion for *yes-no* questions and no *Do* Insertion. Instead, a *yes-no* question is marked by a question particle at the end.
   b. shows that there is no inversion for *Wh* questions, nor is there *Wh* Movement in *Wh* questions.

2. Japanese
   This is an SOV language (unlike English, which is SVO). In other words, V follows its complement rather than vice versa.
   There are postpositions rather than prepositions.
   We can assume, therefore, that this is a head-final language.

   S (IP) ⟶ NP VP I
        (I is the head of IP, so in a head-final language, it follows the complement.)
   NP ⟶ Det N
   VP ⟶ NP PP V
   PP ⟶ NP P

## Review Exercise
Deep structure is shown for all sentences.

1.

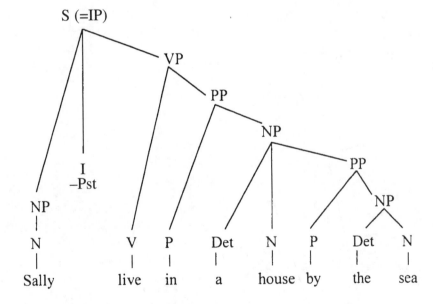

2.

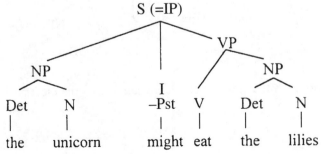

3.

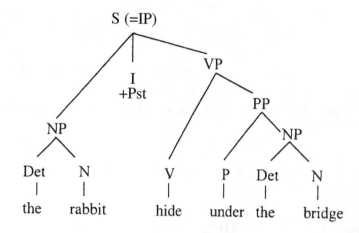

4.

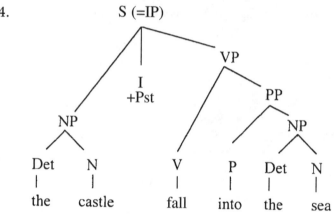

5.

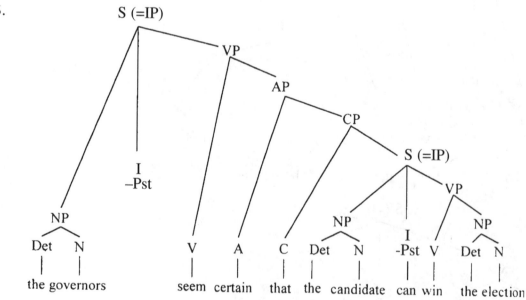

6. *Do* Insertion, Inversion

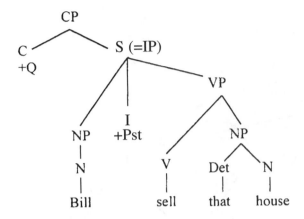

7. *Do* Insertion, Inversion

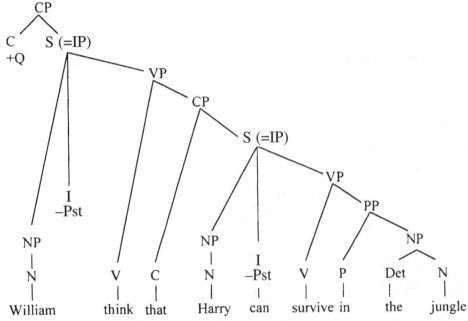

8.

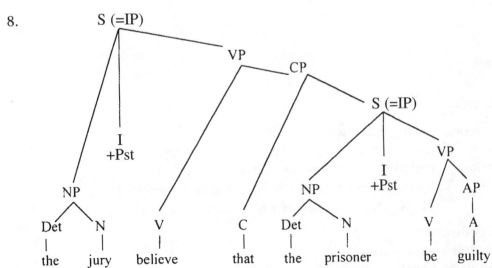

9. NP Movement

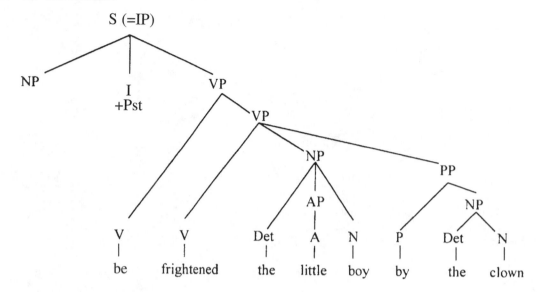

10. *Do* Insertion, Inversion, *Wh* Movement

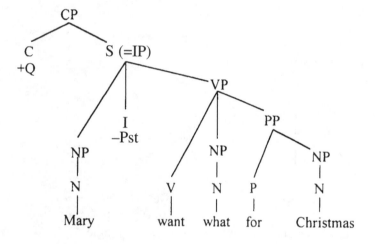

# CHAPTER 6

## Practice 6.1

1.  a. summer

    connotation:    sunny, fun, sticky . . .

    intension:      warmest season of the year

    denotation:     period between summer solstice and autumnal equinox

    extension:      June 21–September 20 in northern hemisphere; December 21–March 20 in southern hemisphere

    b. a linguistics instructor

    connotation:    wise, funny . . .

    intension:      a real or imagined person who teaches linguistics

| | |
|---|---|
| denotation: | any person in the real world who teaches linguistics |
| extension: | your particular professor |

c. grass

| | |
|---|---|
| connotation: | green, sweet-smelling, allergies . . . |
| intension: | green plant that grows on lawns |
| denotation: | narrow-leafed plant |
| extension: | the green stuff in my lawn that is not weeds |

2. Groups A and B are [+living, +human].
   Group A is [+female]. Group B is [–female].
   *grandmother, grandfather, mother,* and *father* are all [+parent].

3.

| ewe | lamb | mare | filly | colt |
|---|---|---|---|---|
| [+animate] | [+animate] | [+animate] | [+animate] | [+animate] |
| [+sheep] | [+sheep] | [+horse] | [+horse] | [+horse] |
| [+adult] | [–adult] | [+adult] | [–adult] | [–adult] |
| [+female] | [–wild] | [+female] | [+female] | [–wild] |
| [–wild] | | [–wild] | [–wild] | |

## Practice 6.2

1. a. grammaticized
   b. graded membership
   c. graded membership; fuzzy concept
   d. grammaticized or graded membership (hour vs. lifetime)
   e. graded membership
   (Answers concerning prototypical members will vary.)

2. Cree
   1–4 are "inalienable." Algonquian languages, of which Cree is one, do not allow an unpossessed form for things that must, by their very nature, belong to someone. Parts of the body and kinship terms are typically inalienable.

3. Swahili
   Singular [m-], plural [wa-]: used for human beings
   Singular [m-], plural [mi-]: used for plants
   Singular [ki-], plural [vi-]: used for inanimate objects

4. German
   Dative *dem* implies a stationary place or location.
   Accusative *das* implies movement to, toward, or into a location.
   German articles contain the idea of movement, whereas English articles (*a, an, the*) contain no such meaning.

## Practice 6.3

1. (answer supplied in the text)
2. paraphrases
3. homophones
4. contradiction

5. entailment
6. antonyms
7. paraphrases
8. contradiction
9. synonyms
10. homophones (both are [stejk])

## Practice 6.4

1. Structural:   a. beer that is cool plus wine (not necessarily cool)
                 b. cool beer and cool wine

2. Structural:   a. The woman is standing at the water cooler now (I may have met her elsewhere.)
                 b. I met the woman while I was standing at the water cooler.

3. Structural:   a. The bill concerns dangerous drugs.
                 b. The drug bill is dangerous.

4. Structural:   a. black ties and white ties
                 b. ties that are two-toned (black and white)

5. Structural:   a. either George and Harry together or Fred alone
                 b. George plus one of the other two (Harry or Fred)

6. Structural:   a. The pictures are in the attic.
                 b. I will be in the attic when I look at the pictures.

7. Lexical:      key to the door, car, answers . . .?

Tree structures for ambiguous phrases in sentences 1, 3, 5, 6:

1. a. 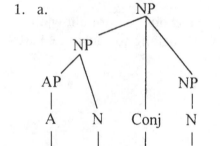 b.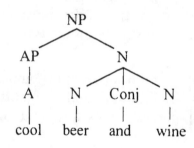

3. a. 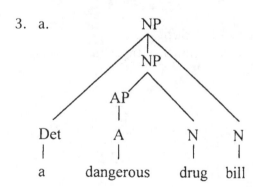 b.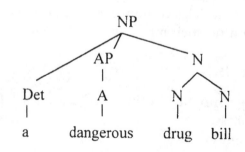

5. a.

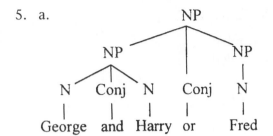

b.

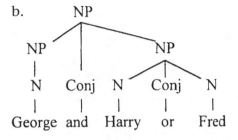

6. a.

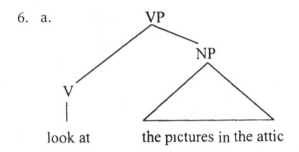

b.

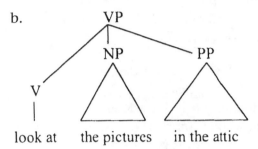

## Practice 6.5

| | NP | Thematic role | Assigned by |
|---|---|---|---|
| 1. | Sarah | agent | drove |
| | that bus | theme | drove |
| | Indianapolis | source | from |
| | Terre Haute | goal | to |
| 2. | children | agent | eating |
| | their ice cream | theme | eating |
| | spoons | instrument | with |
| 3. | you | agent | buy |
| | which shoes | theme | buy |
| | the store | location | at |
| 4. | the cat | theme | chased |
| | a large dog | agent | by |
| | the garden | location | around |
| 5. | the boys | agent | walked |
| | the park | goal | to |
| 6. | Sally | agent | mailed |
| | a parcel | theme | mailed |
| | her nephew | goal/beneficiary | mailed |
| 7. | Bill | agent | leave |
| | what | theme | leave |
| | your house | location | at |
| 8. | the letter | theme | sent |

| NP | Thematic role | Assigned by |
|---|---|---|
| 9. Ginger | agent | scribbled |
| her address | theme | scribbled |
| the paper | location | on |
| a pen | instrument | with |
| 10. the minister | theme | ordained |
| the pulpit | location | in |

## Practice 6.6

1. violates world knowledge
2. ungrammatical
3. violates world knowledge
4. no known referent for *radiculus glautons*
5. violates world knowledge

Sentence 4:   A plant that grows underground? Microscopic creatures? Bacteria? The meaning chosen may affect the meaning of the sentence, and the meaning assumed for the sentence might affect the meaning chosen for the unknown words.

*His mother wants you to be a doctor*:

If you don't know who *he* is, you don't know who *his mother* is and why her wanting you to be a doctor should affect you.

## Practice 6.7

1. Maxim of Quality
2. Maxims of Relation, Quantity, Manner
3. Maxim of Quality
4. Maxims of Relation, Quantity, Manner
5. No violations

### Review Exercises

1. The causative is grammaticized in Burmese. It is indicated by making the first consonant voiceless.

2. Answers will vary.

3.  a.  The witness cannot answer the question because use of *stop* presupposes that the witness has taken or is taking drugs.

    b.  The implicature is not the same. The doctor is asking a genuine information question, whereas the student is making a request.

    c.  The Maxims of Relation and Quantity are being violated. As a result, the implicature of the letter is that the student does not have the necessary academic qualifications for graduate school.

# CHAPTER 7

## Practice 7.1

1. voicing assimilation
2. consonant deletion
3. vowel deletion (apocope)
4. palatalization
5. nasalization, consonant deletion
6. vowel reduction
7. consonant deletion, degemination, vowel deletion (apocope)
8. vowel deletion (syncope), rhotacism
9. epenthesis
10. place of articulation assimilation, degemination (or consonant deletion)
11. vowel deletion (syncope), palatalization
12. voicing assimilation
13. degemination, frication, voicing assimilation
14. total assimilation

Changes from Proto-Germanic [goːdas] to Icelandic [goːðr]:

> frication [d] ⟶ [ð]
> syncope [a] ⟶ Ø  (probably preceded by vowel reduction)
> voicing assimilation [s] ⟶ [z], followed by rhotacism [z] ⟶ [r]

## Practice 7.2

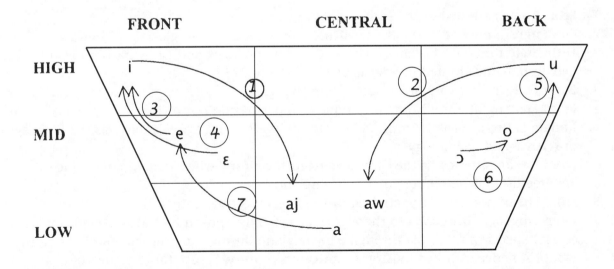

1. Long [i] ⟶ [aj]
2. Long [u] ⟶ [aw]
3. Long [e] ⟶ [i]
4. Long [ɛ] ⟶ [i]
5. Long [o] ⟶ [u]
6. Long [ɔ] ⟶ [o]
7. Long [a] ⟶ [e]

## Practice 7.3

The affix in each case is -(l)ing. The bases are:

1. year
2. duck
3. goose
4. under
5. hire
6. nurse

Words in the first column are generally more common than those in the second column. Words in the first column are diminutive; those in the second column are somewhat pejorative.

a. The affix added l-.

b. The meaning has undergone pejoration. Something small could be considered inferior, leading to the shift in meaning.

c. *Earthling* means 'belonging to Earth'; however, since the word is often used in science fiction when a technologically superior alien is referring to humans on Earth, it can also have the connotation of one who is inferior.

   *Darling* is a diminutive of *dear*, but is used as a term of endearment.

## Practice 7.4

In these examples of sixteenth-century English, a negative was formed by placing *not* after the verb. In contemporary English, *Do* Insertion is mandatory, and the negative is placed between *do* and the verb.

## Practice 7.5

1. Scots Gaelic; attested in the early sixteenth century.
2. Old English; present before the twelfth century, reflecting Anglo-Saxon lifeways.
3. Ultimately from Old Testament Hebrew, by way of Greek and Latin translations of the Old Testament. Attested in English as early as A.D. 825.
4. From Old Norse; a case of adstratum borrowing.
5. From French, after the Norman Conquest. Superstratum borrowing.
6. Middle Latin, ultimately from Arabic. During the Middle Ages, Arabic was the language of science and technology.
7. From Italian; attested in the early seventeenth century, when Italian Renaissance architecture was becoming popular in England.
8. From Greek, via late Latin; attested in the late sixteenth century.
9. From languages belonging to the Algonquian family, spoken by Native Americans in coastal areas from Virginia through New England during early settlement of the north east of America. Attested in early seventeenth century. Substratum borrowing.
10. From Hindi and Marathi; attested in the late eighteenth century, at a time when the British were expanding into India. Substratum borrowing.
11. Ultimately from West African languages, through Spanish/Portuguese. Attested in English in the late sixteenth century, after exploratory voyages along the African coast.
12. This is "New Latin"—a word made from combining a Greek affix (*auto*) and Latin root (*mobile*), a fairly common way of naming new technological inventions.

13. From Tagalog *bundok* 'mountain'; attested in 1909, not long after the Spanish-American War in which the Philippines was acquired as a U.S. territory.

## Practice 7.6

1. broadening
2. amelioration
3. metaphor
4. semantic shift
5. amelioration
6. broadening
7. narrowing
8. broadening
9. pejoration
10. semantic shift/broadening

## Practice 7.7

1. Proto-Algonquian

| Fox | Ojibwa | Menomini | Evidence |
|-----|--------|----------|----------|
| ʃk | ʃk | sk | 1, 6, 9 |
| hk | kk | hk | 2, 7, 10 |
| ht | tt | ʔt | 3, 4, 8 |
| ht | tt | ht | 5, 11, 12 |

| *PA | Fox | Ojibwa | Menomini |
|-----|-----|--------|----------|
| ʔt | ht | tt | ʔt |
| ʃk | ʃk | ʃk | sk |
| hk | hk | kk | hk |
| ht | ht | tt | ht |

2. Arabic

a.

| Position | Syrian | Iraqi | Evidence |
|----------|--------|-------|----------|
| word-initial | d, t | d, θ, ð | 1, 2, 6, 7, 11, 12 |
| word-final | d, t | t, θ, ð | 4, 5, 6, 12 |
| between vowels | d, t | d, θ, ð | 3, 10, 14 |
| after a consonant | d, t | t, θ, ð | 1, 8, 9, 13 |

b. Syrian has only d and t. Iraqi has d, t, θ, ð.

c. Proto-forms: *d, t, θ, ð.

d. Proto d and ð merged to become d in Syrian, but were retained in Iraqi. Proto t and θ merged to become t in Syrian, but were retained in Iraqi.

## Practice 7.8

1. Hypothetical Language Group One:
   Proto-forms:
   1. munto
   2. fumo
   3. pippona
   4. nonka
   5. wusa
   6. fito

Sound changes in Language A:
- Nasalization of V before cluster of nasal + consonant
- Vowel reduction word-finally
- Vowel deletion word-finally in words of more than two syllables
- Deletion of nasal before C

Sound changes in Language B:
- Deletion of nasal before C
- Degemination (3)
- Voicing of consonants word-initially and intervocalically
- Palatalization of glide before high V (5)

2. Hypothetical Language Group Two:
   Proto-forms:           1. puka          2. lizju
   Sound changes in Language A:  Frication intervocalically
   Sound changes in Language B:  Voicing word-initially and intervocalically
   Sound changes in Language C:  l ⟶ r
   Sound changes in Language D:  Vowel deletion word-finally

3. Austronesian
   *PAN. Note: Not all proto-forms can be derived from data presented in the problem set. Alternative acceptable answers are given in parentheses.
   1. anak
   2. sakit
   3. hikat (probably could not be guessed from the data set; *ikat* would be an acceptable answer)
   4. uʀat (could not be guessed from the data set; *urat* or *uzat* would be an acceptable answer)

   Only changes that could be inferred from the data set are listed below.
   Changes in Malay:
   - None, or possibly rhotacism (4) (if PAN were *uzat*)

   Changes in Written Cham:
   - Vowel reduction before word-final [k] (1)
   - Substitution: Word-final stops become glottal stops
   - Substitution: Word-initial s ⟶ h
   - (Possibly rhotacism (4), if PAN were *uzat*)

   Changes in Tsat:
   - Substitution: Word-final stops become glottal stops
   - Deletion of first syllable
   - Development of tones from contact with Chinese, a tone language

4. German dialects
   Note: Proto-forms are derivable from the data set given in the problem. Alternatives are given where proto-forms cannot be derived with certainty from the data set.
   1. makən (or possibly: maːkən)
   2. ik
   3. slaːpən

4.  pʊnt
5.  bejtən or bajtən
6.  dat
7.  tuː

Changes in the Northern dialect:
- Deletion of word-final [n] in verbs
- Possibly compensatory lengthening of vowel (1)

Changes in the Southern dialect:
- Frication following a vowel (1, 2, 3, 5, 6)
- Palatalization (3)
- Affrication of ([+anterior]) voiceless stops word-initially (4, 7)

## Practice 7.9

|     | Sound | Word  |
|-----|-------|-------|
| 1.  | k     | cool  |
| 2.  | p     | lip   |
| 3.  | k/b   | crab  |
| 4.  | g/p   | grip  |
| 5.  | f     | foul  |
| 6.  | h     | home  |
| 7.  | t     | sweet |

## Review Exercises

1.  The Great English Vowel Shift

| Vowel change | Modern English word |
|--------------|---------------------|
| a. oː ⟶ u | noon |
| b. iː ⟶ aj; ə ⟶ Ø/ __# | life |
| c. eː ⟶ i | sweet |
| d. ɔː ⟶ ow | boast |
| e. uː ⟶ aw | gown |

2.  Changes in English since Shakespeare

    a.  SVO is the order in contemporary English.

    Shakespeare used primarily SVO, but the last line of 1 uses SOV.

    b.  Today, *not* goes between the auxiliary and the main verb. (If there is no auxiliary, then *Do* Insertion is mandatory.)

    Shakespeare sometimes placed *not* after the main verb (1, 4), but also used *Do* Insertion (3). In questions with *Do* Insertion, the order could be *do* S (*not*) V or *do* (*not*) S V. This variation suggests that the change to *Do* Insertion was in process in Shakespeare's time.

    c.  Data in 3 and 4 show the variations Shakespeare used in *yes-no* questions. In 3, *Do* Insertion is used, and there is subject-aux Inversion. In 4, there is no *Do* Insertion, and the verb is inverted with the subject.

    d. Second-person singular pronouns *thou, thee,* and *thy* have fallen out of use. Along with these, the *-(e)st* suffix on verbs (*pursuest, didst*) has fallen out of use.

3. Sound changes in Romance

Italian:

- Frication: Voiced stops have become fricatives intervocalically (3).
- Voicing: Voiceless stops have become voiced intervocalically (2).

Spanish:

- Epenthesis: [e] has been inserted word-initially before [s]-stop clusters.
- Voicing + Frication: Voiceless stops became voiced stops intervocalically (2). Intervocalic voiced stops have become fricatives (2, 3).
- Weakening: Geminate [l] weakened to [j] (2).
- Vowel deletion (apocope): Word-final [e] has been deleted. (We can posit an intermediate stage where it was reduced to schwa before being deleted.)

French:

- Epenthesis + Consonant cluster simplification: [e] has been inserted word-initially before [s]-stop clusters, followed by deletion of [s].
- Vowel deletion: Word-final vowels in unstressed syllables have been deleted. (We may assume for 2 that degemination occurred before vowel deletion.)
- In 2, [ut] has become a palatal glide, articulated with rounded lips.
- In 3, the syllable [be] has been deleted with compensatory lengthening of the vowel [i].